D0178524

# GCSE
## Success

# Computer Science

## Sharon Angland

## Exam Practice Workbook

# Fundamentals of algorithms

# Programming 1

# Programming 2

# Programming 3

# Fundamentals of data representation

Contents

# Computer systems

# Fundamentals of computer networks

# Cyber security and ethics

# Practice exam papers

# ASCII table

# Answers

**1** Define the term 'algorithm'. [2 marks]

.................................................................................................................................................

.................................................................................................................................................

**2** Explain the purpose of the algorithm set out in this flowchart. [3 marks]

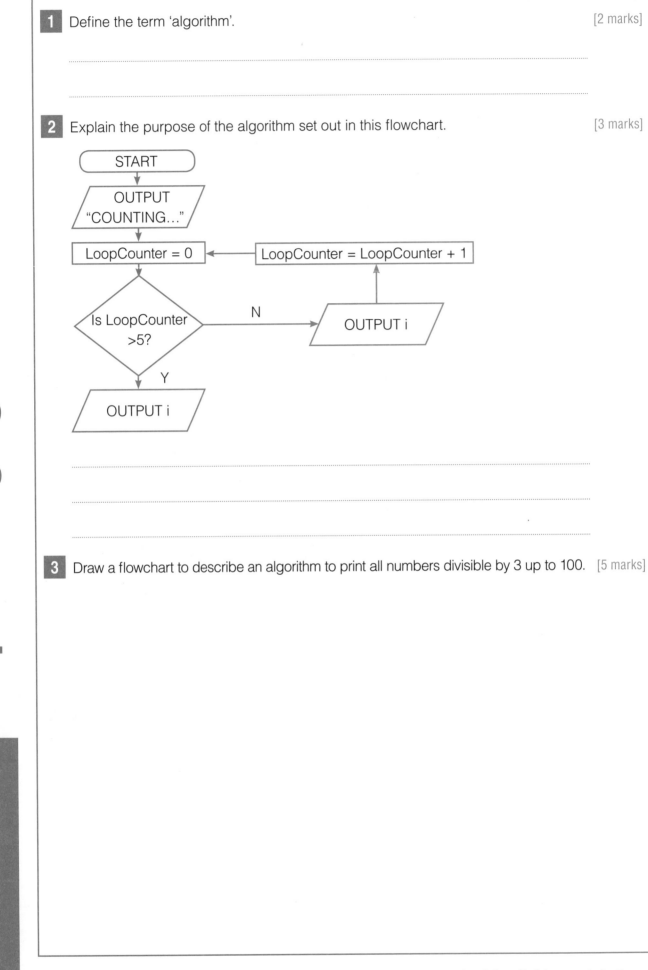

.................................................................................................................................................

.................................................................................................................................................

.................................................................................................................................................

**3** Draw a flowchart to describe an algorithm to print all numbers divisible by 3 up to 100. [5 marks]

**For more help on this topic, see Letts GCSE Computer Science Revision Guide pages 4–5.**

**4** State **two** properties of an algorithm that could be considered when describing it as 'efficient'. [2 marks]

...........................................................................................................................

...........................................................................................................................

**5** A student needs to open and edit a password-protected file.
Put the following steps into the correct order: [5 marks]

Edit Data ......................................................

Save and Close ......................................................

Enter Password ......................................................

Select Program ......................................................

Select File and Open ......................................................

**6** Define 'iteration' in the context of designing a program structure. [1 mark]

...........................................................................................................................

**7** How would a programmer use decomposition when given an initial project brief? [2 marks]

...........................................................................................................................

...........................................................................................................................

**8** How might we use abstraction to create a clearer 'model' of a problem? [2 marks]

...........................................................................................................................

...........................................................................................................................

**9** Explain how a trace table is used to test a computer program to check for early errors. [2 marks]

...........................................................................................................................

...........................................................................................................................

...........................................................................................................................

**Representing algorithms**

**Module 1**

**For more help on this topic, see Letts GCSE Computer Science Revision Guide pages 4–5.**

1 Explain the steps involved in a binary search. [4 marks]

.................................................................................................................................................................

.................................................................................................................................................................

.................................................................................................................................................................

.................................................................................................................................................................

2 Explain how a linear search looks at a data source. [2 marks]

.................................................................................................................................................................

.................................................................................................................................................................

3 Identify what type of search this is. [1 mark]

```
ClassList= ["Alex", "Riley", "Chris", "Bailey", "Jamie"]
INPUT A #name you're looking for
FOREACH [item in list]:
    IF [item] == A,
        OUTPUT result stop search
    ELSE
        RETURN
END
```

.................................................................................................................................................................

4 Linear search is often also known as 'brute force' searching.

Why is this? [1 mark]

.................................................................................................................................................................

.................................................................................................................................................................

5 Why does a binary search require a sorted dataset? [3 marks]

.................................................................................................................................................................

.................................................................................................................................................................

.................................................................................................................................................................

.................................................................................................................................................................

**For more help on this topic, see Letts GCSE Computer Science Revision Guide pages 6–7.**

**6** Explain when a linear search might be more efficient than a binary search. [2 marks]

........................................................................................................

........................................................................................................

**7** At first glance, which type of search would be the most appropriate for the following data?

Give a reason for your answer. [2 marks]

> I want to find if there are any '9's in the list:
>
> 1,2,3,4,5,6,7,8,9,10,11,12

........................................................................................................

........................................................................................................

**8** Which would be the most appropriate type of search for the following data?

Give a reason for your answer. [2 marks]

> I want to find if there are any Hussains in the class:
>
> "Adams", "Banks", "Kelly", "Madsen", "Lisson", "Hepworth"

........................................................................................................

........................................................................................................

**For more help on this topic, see Letts GCSE Computer Science Revision Guide pages 6–7.**

**1** Which of the following processes describes merge sort? Tick **one** option. [1 mark]

**A** Repeatedly splits the data in half until each 'list' contains only a single data item. Then, having broken it into smaller parts, it repeatedly combines these 'lists' back together, this time putting them in their required order (ascending or descending in value). ☐

**B** Compares the first two items, checks which one is larger and swaps them if necessary so that the larger is first. Then it checks the next pair, and so on. ☐

**2** Use a bubble sort to sort the dataset (6,2,4,1,8) in ascending order. Show your working and state the number of steps required. [4 marks]

........................................................................................................................

........................................................................................................................

........................................................................................................................

........................................................................................................................

........................................................................................................................

........................................................................................................................

**3** Complete the merge sort example shown. [3 marks]

| 4 | 1 | 9 | 6 |

| 4 | 1 |     | 6 |

| 4 |

**For more help on this topic, see Letts GCSE Computer Science Revision Guide pages 8–9.**

**1** What is a 'Boolean data type'?                                                           [1 mark]

...................................................................................................................................

**2** Explain what type of data a telephone number is.                                         [3 marks]

...................................................................................................................................

...................................................................................................................................

**3** What is a 'variable'?                                                                     [3 marks]

...................................................................................................................................

...................................................................................................................................

**4** What is the value of a at the end of this code segment?                                  [1 mark]

```
a = 0
for i = 1 to 5
    a = a+1
next i
print a
```

...................................................................................................................................

**5** What does the phrase 'constant declaration' mean, and how is it different from
declaring a variable?                                                                          [4 marks]

...................................................................................................................................

...................................................................................................................................

...................................................................................................................................

**6** 'Repeat' instructions like the one below are an example of which technique?              [1 mark]
(NB fd = 'forward'; 'rt' = 'right' followed by the degrees to turn)

Repeat 360 [fd 1 rt 1]

...................................................................................................................................

**7** Identify the benefit to the programmer of iteration in a code.                           [4 marks]

...................................................................................................................................

...................................................................................................................................

...................................................................................................................................

**For more help on this topic, see Letts GCSE Computer Science Revision Guide pages 12–13.**

Data types

Module 4

**1** Give a definition of 'pseudocode'. [2 marks]

........................................................................................................................................

........................................................................................................................................

........................................................................................................................................

**2** Write the pseudocode for a simple algorithm that is used to process data entered by a class teacher. It prints 'passed' if a student's mark is above 30, and 'did not pass' if it isn't. [2 marks]

........................................................................................................................................

........................................................................................................................................

........................................................................................................................................

........................................................................................................................................

........................................................................................................................................

**3** Explain what the following code does. [3 marks]

```
n=0
while n<=100
    display n
    n=n+1
endwhile
```

........................................................................................................................................

........................................................................................................................................

**For more help on this topic, see Letts GCSE Computer Science Revision Guide pages 14–15.**

**4** Explain what the following code does. [3 marks]

```
input startnumber, finish
if startnumber > finish
      print error message
else
      for n=startnumber to finishnumber
          print n
      next
endif
```

**5** Write the pseudocode to take three numbers as input and print the sum and product of those numbers. [3 marks]

**For more help on this topic, see Letts GCSE Computer Science Revision Guide pages 14–15.**

Module 5

**1** Write a simple program to multiply two user input numbers together, and print the result. [1 mark]

....................................................................................................................................

....................................................................................................................................

....................................................................................................................................

....................................................................................................................................

**2** Explain why the following two codes would display and produce different results. [3 marks]

| Code 1 | Code 2 |
|---|---|
| a = 13 | a = 13 |
| b = 2 | b = 2 |
| c = INT(a/b) | c = FLOAT(a/b) |
| print c | print c |

....................................................................................................................................

....................................................................................................................................

....................................................................................................................................

....................................................................................................................................

....................................................................................................................................

**3** Explain why the calculation in this program would cause a problem. [1 mark]

```
input Name
input Age
Score =
Name*Age
Print Score
```

....................................................................................................................................

....................................................................................................................................

....................................................................................................................................

**For more help on this topic, see Letts GCSE Computer Science Revision Guide pages 16–17.**

4 The following code aims to work out overtime pay.

Describe why it is incorrect. [2 marks]

```
Input EmployeeName
Input HoursWorked
Input HourRate
Input OvertimeWorked
Input OvertimeRate
pay = (HoursWorked / HourRate) + (OvertimeWorked * OvertimeRate)
print pay
End
```

.................................................................................................................

.................................................................................................................

5 State what the output and result of this code would be. [2 marks]

```
a = 15
b = 23
IF a < 10 AND b < 50
    print "Class Dismissed"
ELSE
    print "Extra Homework!"
ENDIF
```

.................................................................................................................

.................................................................................................................

6 If line three in question 5 is changed to: [2 marks]

```
IF a >= 10 AND b < 50
    print "Class Dismissed"
```

what will be the result, and why?

.................................................................................................................

.................................................................................................................

**For more help on this topic, see Letts GCSE Computer Science Revision Guide pages 16–17.**

1 What do the following flowchart symbols mean? [4 marks]

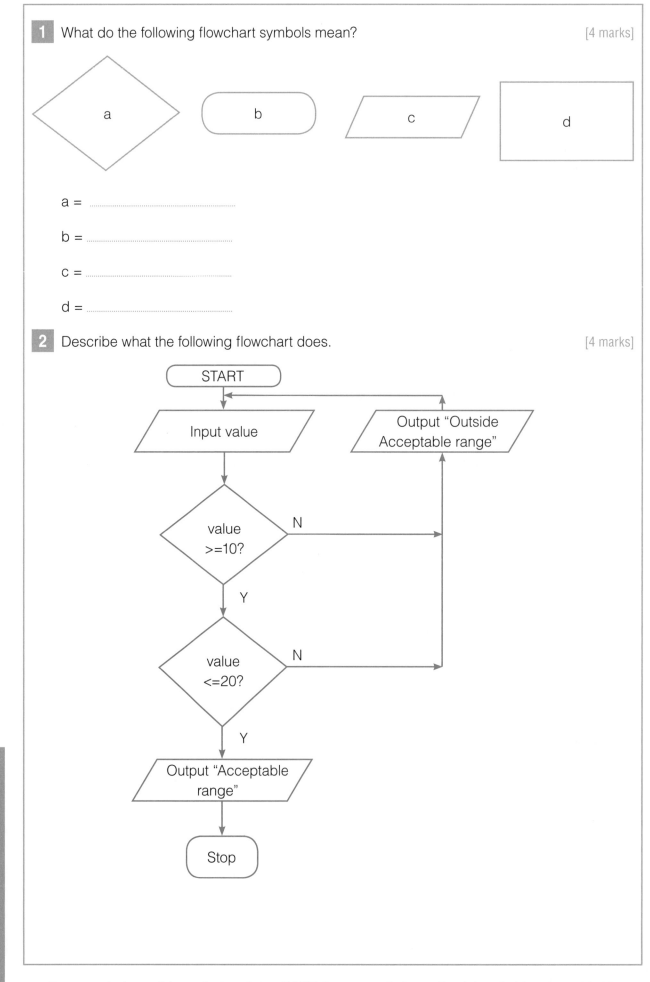

a =  .........................................................

b =  .........................................................

c =  .........................................................

d =  .........................................................

2 Describe what the following flowchart does. [4 marks]

**For more help on this topic, see Letts GCSE Computer Science Revision Guide pages 18–19.**

_____

_____

_____

_____

_____

**3** Put the flowchart elements below in the correct order to monitor the
temperature in a greenhouse.                                    [2 marks]

```
  ◇ TEMP ≤        READ          PRINT "CLOSE      PRINT "TEMP
    15DEG?        TEMPERATURE   WINDOWS!"         FINE!"

         STOP                   START
```

**For more help on this topic, see Letts GCSE Computer Science Revision Guide pages 18–19.**

1 Black and white bitmap images can be encoded using 1 to represent white and 0 to represent black in a two-dimensional array. Show the two dimensional array for the capital letter C where the array is 4 pixels by 4 pixels. [2 marks]

2 In programming, what are 'data structures'? [2 marks]

3 If a list contains the following elements, what would be output by the command `print(text[2])` if the array count starts at [0]? Give a reason for your answer. [2 marks]

text = ["apples"; "oranges"; "pears"; "bananas"]

4 Is this acceptable data for an array? Give a reason for your answer. [2 marks]

names = ["Max","Khali",22,"Sam")

5 If a two-dimensional array is defined as below, identify how many elements are contained within it. [2 marks]

myArray(6,6)

6 In the list below, identify the item at index point [5] if the index starts at [0]. [1 mark]

(1,2,3,4,5,6,7,8,9)

7 What do programmers mean when they describe an array as 'static'? [1 mark]

**For more help on this topic, see Letts GCSE Computer Science Revision Guide pages 22–23.**

**1** Describe what this code would do. [4 marks]

```
file = open("contacts.csv", "a")
name = input("Please enter name.")
phone = input("Please enter phone number.")
file.write(name + "," + phone + "\n")
```

....................................................................................................................................

....................................................................................................................................

**2** Describe **two** ways external data can be collected. [2 marks]

....................................................................................................................................

....................................................................................................................................

**3** Describe how an index aids file handling. [2 marks]

....................................................................................................................................

....................................................................................................................................

**4** Explain why it is possible for someone to enter a chatroom for 20-year-olds
and be only 15. [2 marks]

....................................................................................................................................

....................................................................................................................................

**5** Complete the code below to add a new name to a class list. [2 marks]

```
file = open("classlist.csv", "a")

...................... = input("Please enter name.")

file. ...................... (name + ","+ "\n")
```

**6** If a file is opened, edited, saved and closed on a daily basis, identify a
limitation of this method and a possible solution. [2 marks]

....................................................................................................................................

....................................................................................................................................

....................................................................................................................................

**For more help on this topic, see Letts GCSE Computer Science Revision Guide pages 24–25.**

Module 9

**1** Define the data type 'string'. [2 marks]

....................................................................................................................................................................

....................................................................................................................................................................

**2** Complete the following table to show which data you would store as an integer and which you would store as a string.

Tick **one** box in each row. [4 marks]

| Data type | Store as an integer | Store as a string |
|---|---|---|
| Steve | | |
| 15 | | |
| 007 | | |
| 2010 | | |
| 10.2 | | |
| 01501 2987659 | | |

**3** If the following variables are given string values, what would be the result when they were concatenated in the same order in which they were entered?

Give a reason for your answer. [2 marks]

```
one = "fish"
two = "chips"
three = "mushy peas"
```

....................................................................................................................................................................

....................................................................................................................................................................

**4** A string can also be an array of characters:

```
one = ["f", "i", "s", "h"]
```

If a function returns the numeric character code, and the character code for one[1] is 105 and the character code for one[3] is 104, what is the character code for one[0]? [1 mark]

....................................................................................................................................................................

**5** Explain why a character encoding system uses a different code for upper- and lowercase letters. [1 mark]

....................................................................................................................................................................

....................................................................................................................................................................

**For more help on this topic, see Letts GCSE Computer Science Revision Guide pages 26–27.**

**1** Explain the difference between a random number and a pseudorandom number. [2 marks]

**2** Describe **two** modern uses of computer-generated random numbers. [2 marks]

**3** Explain what the following code does. How does it use the random feature within the language? [4 marks]

```
import random
My _ number = random.randint(1, 100)
guess = int(input("Take a guess: "))
tries = 1

# guessing loop
while guess != Mynumber:
    if guess > Mynumber:
       print("Too high!")
    else:
       print("Too low!")
    endif
    guess = int(input("What is your guess: "))
    tries += 1
endwhile
print("You got it!  The number was", Mynumber)
print("And it only took you", guesses, "tries!\n")
```

**For more help on this topic, see Letts GCSE Computer Science Revision Guide pages 28–29.**

**Module 11**

1   Explain the difference between a flat file and a relational database. Support your
    answer with examples.                                                              [4 marks]

    ........................................................................................................................

    ........................................................................................................................

    ........................................................................................................................

2   What is the role of a primary key?                                                 [1 mark]

    ........................................................................................................................

3   Giving examples, what is the difference between 'structured' and 'unstructured' data?   [4 marks]

    ........................................................................................................................

    ........................................................................................................................

    ........................................................................................................................

4   State the purpose of a database report.                                            [1 mark]

    ........................................................................................................................

5   Use the table below to answer the following questions.

| StockList | | | | |
|---|---|---|---|---|
| **Product ID** | **Product type** | **Colour** | **Size** | **Cost** |
| **A** 569875 | T-shirt | Blue | S | £14.99 |
| **B** 258649 | Trainers | Black | 6 | £29.99 |
| **C** 333548 | Hoodie | Red | M | £29.99 |
| **D** 335948 | Shirt | White | M | £12.99 |
| **E** 798994 | Socks | White | 5 | £6.99 |
| **F** 222687 | Shirt | Blue | M | £12.99 |

    What would be the outcome of these SQL searches?

    (a)
    ```
    SELECT * FROM StockList
    WHERE Size='M'
    AND Colour='White'
    ```
    ............................................................    [1 mark]

    (b)
    ```
    SELECT * FROM StockList
    WHERE Size='M'
    AND ProductType='Shirt'
    ```
    ............................................................    [2 marks]

    (c)
    ```
    SELECT * FROM StockList
    WHERE Cost<£20.00
    ```
    ............................................................    [4 marks]

**For more help on this topic, see Letts GCSE Computer Science Revision Guide pages 30–31.**

**1** Give **three** reasons why using a structured approach to their code will benefit a programmer. [3 marks]

**2** Within structured programming, good programmers plan what they intend to do, then comment the code as it is constructed. In this context, what is a comment? Give an example. [2 marks]

**3** Describe the **three** types of translation programming software and provide a brief description of each. [6 marks]

**4** Describe the steps a programmer can take to make the code they write easier for another programmer to follow. [4 marks]

1.

2.

3.

4.

For more help on this topic, see Letts GCSE Computer Science Revision Guide pages 34–35.

**1** Name a parameter within this function. [1 mark]

```
FUNCTION Test1(name, value)
    IF name[1] = value
        RETURN true
    ELSE
        RETURN false
    ENDIF
ENDFUNCTION
```

**2** Describe **two** examples of using subroutines in a program. [2 marks]

**3** A school is developing a part of its website to allow parents and students to upload images. They need a subroutine that would check that the image is within the maximum size allowed (1 MB) before uploading only those that are the right size.

Write a pseudocode subroutine that would do this. [6 marks]

**4** Four separate subroutines have been written to control a robot in a factory:

FD (x) moves the robot x squares forwards
LT (x) turns the robot x degrees left
RT (x) turns the robot x degrees right
Obstacle() is a Boolean response to the status of the robot

**For more help on this topic, see Letts GCSE Computer Science Revision Guide pages 36–37.**

**(a)** What would be the path of the robot through the grid below if the following code was executed? [1 mark]

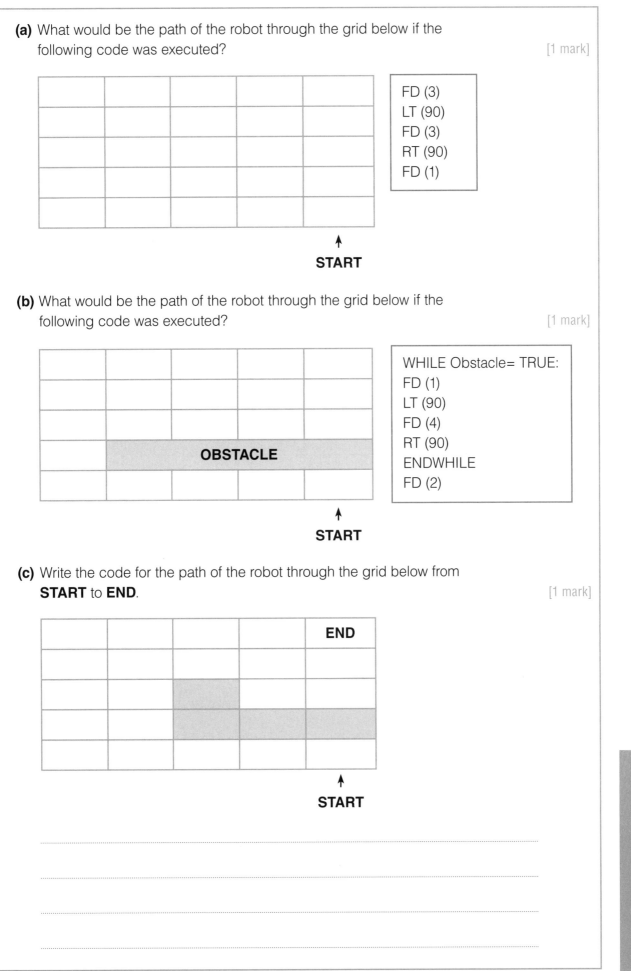

```
FD (3)
LT (90)
FD (3)
RT (90)
FD (1)
```

START

**(b)** What would be the path of the robot through the grid below if the following code was executed? [1 mark]

OBSTACLE

```
WHILE Obstacle= TRUE:
FD (1)
LT (90)
FD (4)
RT (90)
ENDWHILE
FD (2)
```

START

**(c)** Write the code for the path of the robot through the grid below from **START** to **END**. [1 mark]

END

START

....................................................................................................................................................

....................................................................................................................................................

....................................................................................................................................................

....................................................................................................................................................

**For more help on this topic, see Letts GCSE Computer Science Revision Guide pages 36–37.**

1 A program is only as good as its data. Explain how validation and verification can help ensure that the data is as 'good' as possible. [6 marks]

2 Describe **one** method of validation used by online surveys to help them manage the quality of their data. [2 marks]

3 Validation is required for the data in the parameters for the function below:

Function WorkingTime (TimeIn,TimeOut)

Set a test, and show an example of invalid data. [2 marks]

4 Give **two** reasons why programmers test their code. [2 marks]

1.

2.

5 A program requires a date of birth from the 20th century to be entered. Provide normal, extreme and erroneous test data examples in the format DD/MM/YYYY. [3 marks]

**For more help on this topic, see Letts GCSE Computer Science Revision Guide pages 38–39.**

**1** Explain why programmers use hexadecimal instead of binary. [3 marks]

.......................................................................................................................................

.......................................................................................................................................

**2** What is the decimal representation of the hexadecimal number A2?

Show your working. [2 marks]

.......................................................................................................................................

.......................................................................................................................................

.......................................................................................................................................

**3** What is the binary result of 00000111 + 00000111?

Show your working. [2 marks]

.......................................................................................................................................

.......................................................................................................................................

.......................................................................................................................................

**4** What is the hexadecimal representation of 256?

Show your working. [2 marks]

.......................................................................................................................................

.......................................................................................................................................

.......................................................................................................................................

.......................................................................................................................................

**For more help on this topic, see Letts GCSE Computer Science Revision Guide pages 42–43.**

1   Each unit in binary is called a 'bit', and a single bit in binary can represent one of two numbers, 0 and 1.

How many numbers can be represented by:

(a) 3 bits? ............................................... [1 mark]

(b) 8 bits? ............................................... [1 mark]

(c) 12 bits? ............................................... [1 mark]

2   Describe how 1 bit per pixel can be used to represent this image. [1 mark]

......................................................................................................

......................................................................................................

3   If 8 bits are a byte, what are 4 bits? [1 mark]

......................................................................................................

4   If a kilobyte is 1024 bytes and a megabyte (MB) is 1024 kilobytes,
fill in the gaps for the following sizes. [2 marks]

A gigabyte (GB) is 1024 ............................................... .

A terabyte (TB) is 1024 ............................................... .

5   If a robot has a 4-bit instruction set, how many individual different instructions can it operate?

Give a reason for your answer. [2 marks]

......................................................................................................

......................................................................................................

**For more help on this topic, see Letts GCSE Computer Science Revision Guide pages 44–45.**

**6** On a computer monitor, state how many colours are displayed by 8-bit colour. [1 mark]

......................................................

**7** Define 'colour depth' and state how it affects file size. [2 marks]

......................................................

......................................................

......................................................

**8** Give a significant disadvantage of ASCII code that led to the development of Unicode. [2 marks]

......................................................

......................................................

......................................................

......................................................

......................................................

**For more help on this topic, see Letts GCSE Computer Science Revision Guide pages 44–45.**

**1** Sound, which is naturally analogue, is converted into a digital format through sampling. What is this process, and what impact does the sample rate have on file size? [4 marks]

...........................................................................................................................................................................

...........................................................................................................................................................................

...........................................................................................................................................................................

...........................................................................................................................................................................

...........................................................................................................................................................................

**2** Define what 'bit depth' is and what impact it has on the quality of the sound. [2 marks]

...........................................................................................................................................................................

...........................................................................................................................................................................

**3** Two versions of the same tune, with the same sample rate, have very different file sizes. Explain why tune.wav is 50.4 MB and tune.mp3 is 3.43 MB. [2 marks]

...........................................................................................................................................................................

...........................................................................................................................................................................

**4** State what is meant by 'resolution' of a monitor. Explain what impact resolution has on the quality of graphics displayed. [4 marks]

...........................................................................................................................................................................

...........................................................................................................................................................................

...........................................................................................................................................................................

**5** A JPEG file format uses lossy compression. Explain what this means for both the quality of the image and the size of the file. [3 marks]

...........................................................................................................................................................................

...........................................................................................................................................................................

**6** What is a 'pixel'? [2 marks]

...........................................................................................................................................................................

...........................................................................................................................................................................

...........................................................................................................................................................................

**For more help on this topic, see Letts GCSE Computer Science Revision Guide pages 46–47.**

**1** Describe what a 'Huffman tree' is and what purpose it serves.                    [2 marks]

..................................................................................................................

..................................................................................................................

..................................................................................................................

**2** Describe what 'Run Length Encoding (RLE)' is.                                    [2 marks]

..................................................................................................................

..................................................................................................................

..................................................................................................................

**3** Describe an example type of file where RLE is commonly used.                     [1 mark]

..................................................................................................................

..................................................................................................................

**4** A Huffman tree for the text 2012 LONDON OLYMPICS is shown below.

Complete the missing sections.                                                         [5 marks]

**For more help on this topic, see Letts GCSE Computer Science Revision Guide pages 48–49.**

Data compression

Module 19

1 A client complains that their laptop computer is running very slowly, even though their anti-virus software is up to date.

Give **two** examples of how utility software could help free up some space on the hard drive.

[2 marks]

.................................................................................................................................

.................................................................................................................................

2 On the motherboard, which element is used to connect different components in the CPU?

Tick **one** option.

[1 mark]

Port ☐

Firewire ☐

Network ☐

Bus ☐

3 Define what 'hardware' is.

[1 mark]

.................................................................................................................................

.................................................................................................................................

4 A client complains that their laptop is running very slowly, even though their anti-virus software is up to date, and they do not have a lot of data on their hard disk.

How could adding to the memory in the laptop help to solve this?

[2 marks]

.................................................................................................................................

.................................................................................................................................

.................................................................................................................................

.................................................................................................................................

**For more help on this topic, see Letts GCSE Computer Science Revision Guide pages 52–53.**

**5** Complete the following truth table for an OR logic gate. [2 marks]

| A | B | A OR B |
|---|---|--------|
| 0 | 0 | |
| 0 | 1 | |
| 1 | 0 | |
| 1 | 1 | |

**6** The image below is a black and white image of 25 pixels.

Explain why 25 bits would be needed to represent this image. [2 marks]

.....................................................................................................................................................

.....................................................................................................................................................

.....................................................................................................................................................

.....................................................................................................................................................

**For more help on this topic, see Letts GCSE Computer Science Revision Guide pages 52–53.**

**1** System software and application software are two different types of software. Give **one** example of application software. [1 mark]

.....................................................................................................................................................

**2** Which of the following is an example of a utility program?

Tick **one** option. [1 mark]

Spreadsheet ☐

Anti-virus checker ☐

Internet browser ☐

**3** What is 'open source software'? [1 mark]

.....................................................................................................................................................

**4** Explain the main difference between a Command Line Interface (CLI) and a Graphical User Interface (GUI). [4 marks]

.....................................................................................................................................................

.....................................................................................................................................................

.....................................................................................................................................................

.....................................................................................................................................................

**5** Explain what the purpose of an operating system is. [5 marks]

.....................................................................................................................................................

.....................................................................................................................................................

.....................................................................................................................................................

.....................................................................................................................................................

.....................................................................................................................................................

**6** Describe what a device driver does. [2 marks]

.....................................................................................................................................................

.....................................................................................................................................................

.....................................................................................................................................................

**For more help on this topic, see Letts GCSE Computer Science Revision Guide pages 54–55.**

**1** What is the difference between volatile and non-volatile memory?

Give an example of each. [3 marks]

........................................................................................................................

........................................................................................................................

........................................................................................................................

**2** State what a 'Von Neumann bottleneck' is. [1 mark]

........................................................................................................................

........................................................................................................................

**3** Describe briefly the 'fetch-execute cycle'. [1 mark]

........................................................................................................................

........................................................................................................................

**4** Why are both RAM and ROM unsuitable alternatives to secondary storage? [2 marks]

........................................................................................................................

........................................................................................................................

**5** Below are three different types of memory.

Tick the fastest from these types of memory. [1 mark]

Level 1 cache ☐

RAM ☐

Level 2 cache ☐

**For more help on this topic, see Letts GCSE Computer Science Revision Guide pages 56–57.**

**6** When might a computer use virtual memory? [1 mark]

......................................................................................................................................

......................................................................................................................................

**7** Describe why a computer uses cache memory. [2 marks]

......................................................................................................................................

......................................................................................................................................

**8** What is a 'bus' on a motherboard? [1 mark]

......................................................................................................................................

**9** In addition to the CPU clock speed, name **two** factors that can affect the CPU's
performance. [2 marks]

......................................................................................................................................

......................................................................................................................................

......................................................................................................................................

......................................................................................................................................

**For more help on this topic, see Letts GCSE Computer Science Revision Guide pages 56–57.**

**1** In addition to solid state and magnetic storage, name a type of secondary storage and give an example. [2 marks]

........................................................................................................................

**2** What is the difference between a '–R' and '–RW' in relation to an optional disc? [2 marks]

........................................................................................................................

........................................................................................................................

........................................................................................................................

**3** A small organisation wants to transfer all its data onto a cloud storage plan. Discuss the advantages and disadvantages of this option. [8 marks]

........................................................................................................................

........................................................................................................................

........................................................................................................................

........................................................................................................................

........................................................................................................................

........................................................................................................................

........................................................................................................................

........................................................................................................................

**4** Explain, using an example, what is an 'embedded system' is. [2 marks]

........................................................................................................................

........................................................................................................................

........................................................................................................................

........................................................................................................................

**5** Tablet computers and mobile phones tend to use solid state media for storage rather than hard drives. Describe **two** reasons, other than cost and capacity, why solid state is used. [4 marks]

........................................................................................................................

........................................................................................................................

........................................................................................................................

**For more help on this topic, see Letts GCSE Computer Science Revision Guide pages 58–59.**

Secondary storage

Module 23

**1** What is a 'Personal Area Network (PAN)'? [2 marks]

.................................................................................................................................................

.................................................................................................................................................

**2** Explain the difference between a local area network (LAN) and a wide area network (WAN). Give an example of a situation where each might be used. [4 marks]

.................................................................................................................................................

.................................................................................................................................................

.................................................................................................................................................

.................................................................................................................................................

**3** Which type of networking (wired or wireless) would you recommend for a small office with four people who use laptops and share a printer? Explain your answer. [5 marks]

.................................................................................................................................................

.................................................................................................................................................

.................................................................................................................................................

.................................................................................................................................................

.................................................................................................................................................

**4** "Schools should ban all onsite wireless connectivity for students."
Discuss this statement. [8 marks]

.................................................................................................................................................

.................................................................................................................................................

.................................................................................................................................................

.................................................................................................................................................

.................................................................................................................................................

.................................................................................................................................................

.................................................................................................................................................

.................................................................................................................................................

**For more help on this topic, see Letts GCSE Computer Science Revision Guide pages 62–63.**

**1** Describe the differences between a star network topology and a mesh network topology. [4 marks]

..................................................................................................................................................

..................................................................................................................................................

..................................................................................................................................................

..................................................................................................................................................

**2** Draw an example of a ring network topology, showing clearly each of the components: printer, storage/server, three workstations. [5 marks]

**3** Describe how MAC address filtering supports security on a network. [3 marks]

..................................................................................................................................................

..................................................................................................................................................

..................................................................................................................................................

**4** Identify the difference between whitelist and blacklist filtering. Explain which is the more secure. Explain which is more flexible. [4 marks]

..................................................................................................................................................

..................................................................................................................................................

..................................................................................................................................................

..................................................................................................................................................

**5** Why is a ring network vulnerable to system failure? [2 marks]

..................................................................................................................................................

..................................................................................................................................................

**Network topology**

**Module 25**

**For more help on this topic, see Letts GCSE Computer Science Revision Guide pages 64–65.**

1 Draw a diagram identifying the basic four layers of the Internet. [4 marks]

2 Describe the purpose of the 'Transport Layer' of the Internet. [2 marks]

.......................................................................................................................................................

.......................................................................................................................................................

.......................................................................................................................................................

.......................................................................................................................................................

3 In online networks there are a number of protocols. What is a 'protocol'? [2 marks]

.......................................................................................................................................................

.......................................................................................................................................................

.......................................................................................................................................................

4 Client-server communication:
Tick **one** option in each case, showing whether the action would take place at the
client end, server end or both. [3 marks]

| Action | CLIENT | SERVER | BOTH |
|---|---|---|---|
| Starting handshake | | | |
| Displaying HTML pages | | | |
| Receiving messages | | | |

5 Describe what the 'client-server model' is. [2 marks]

.......................................................................................................................................................

.......................................................................................................................................................

6 What elements may be found on the 'application layer' of the 4-layer Internet model?
What purpose does the application layer serve? [2 marks]

.......................................................................................................................................................

.......................................................................................................................................................

.......................................................................................................................................................

**For more help on this topic, see Letts GCSE Computer Science Revision Guide pages 66–67.**

**1** In the context of cyber security, what is a 'Trojan horse'? [2 marks]

**2** What is 'good password practice' in terms of security? Give **four** examples. [4 marks]

   **1.**

   **2.**

   **3.**

   **4.**

**3** Explain why, when you forget your password, the company holding your account should send you a link to reset your password, not a copy of your password. [4 marks]

**4** What is 'adware' and is it dangerous to your computer? [2 marks]

**5** Describe **three** examples of phishing. [3 marks]

**6** How is social engineering a threat to data security? [4 marks]

**For more help on this topic, see Letts GCSE Computer Science Revision Guide pages 70–71.**

Definition, purpose and threat

Module 27

**7** How is 'malware' a threat to a network? [2 marks]

.......................................................................................................................................

.......................................................................................................................................

.......................................................................................................................................

.......................................................................................................................................

**8** Why do networks have access levels for users?

Tick **one** option. [1 mark]

To give everyone access to download any files they want. ☐

To control the access different users have to information. ☐

To let the network manager know who is doing what on the network. ☐

**9** What is Distributed Denial of Service (DDOS)? Describe what it does to a web server. [4 marks]

.......................................................................................................................................

.......................................................................................................................................

.......................................................................................................................................

.......................................................................................................................................

.......................................................................................................................................

**10** Describe how poor network policies can endanger the security of a network. [2 marks]

.......................................................................................................................................

.......................................................................................................................................

.......................................................................................................................................

.......................................................................................................................................

**11** Why is it important to keep all software up to date, especially on a device that is attached to the Internet? [4 marks]

.......................................................................................................................................

.......................................................................................................................................

.......................................................................................................................................

.......................................................................................................................................

**For more help on this topic, see Letts GCSE Computer Science Revision Guide pages 70–71.**

**1** Define the term 'encryption'. [2 marks]

...................................................................................................................................................

...................................................................................................................................................

**2** What is the difference between encryption and encoding? Explain with examples. [4 marks]

...................................................................................................................................................

...................................................................................................................................................

...................................................................................................................................................

...................................................................................................................................................

**3** Give **four** reasons why encryption is so important to online communication. [4 marks]

1. ...............................................................................................................................................

2. ...............................................................................................................................................

3. ...............................................................................................................................................

4. ...............................................................................................................................................

**4** What does the 's' in https stand for? [1 mark]

...................................................................................................................................................

**5** What is a 'private key', and how does it support secure communication? [4 marks]

...................................................................................................................................................

...................................................................................................................................................

...................................................................................................................................................

...................................................................................................................................................

**6** Modern organisations are spending increasing amounts of money on cyber security. This includes penetration testing, which is an attack by an organisation on its own computer system to identify weak points. What is the difference between black and white box penetration testing? [4 marks]

...................................................................................................................................................

...................................................................................................................................................

...................................................................................................................................................

...................................................................................................................................................

**For more help on this topic, see Letts GCSE Computer Science Revision Guide pages 72–73.**

7 Identify **two** advantages and **two** disadvantages of a basic password system. [4 marks]

........................................................................................................................

........................................................................................................................

........................................................................................................................

........................................................................................................................

8 What is the purpose of CAPTCHA elements on web forms? [2 marks]

........................................................................................................................

........................................................................................................................

9 Name **two** potential disadvantages of CAPTCHA. [2 marks]

........................................................................................................................

........................................................................................................................

........................................................................................................................

10 **(a)** Define the term 'biometrics'. [3 marks]

........................................................................................................................

........................................................................................................................

........................................................................................................................

........................................................................................................................

**(b)** Explain how biometrics can be a higher level of security than basic passwords. [4 marks]

........................................................................................................................

........................................................................................................................

........................................................................................................................

........................................................................................................................

........................................................................................................................

........................................................................................................................

**For more help on this topic, see Letts GCSE Computer Science Revision Guide pages 72–73.**

**1** The EU 'right to be forgotten' ruling allows individuals to request online data held about them to be erased. Many are concerned however that this may aid criminal activities. Whose rights should be prioritised? Give reasons for your answer. [6 marks]

.................................................................................................................................

.................................................................................................................................

.................................................................................................................................

.................................................................................................................................

.................................................................................................................................

.................................................................................................................................

.................................................................................................................................

**2** Discuss whether the 'Internet of Things' is a good idea. [6 marks]

.................................................................................................................................

.................................................................................................................................

.................................................................................................................................

.................................................................................................................................

.................................................................................................................................

.................................................................................................................................

.................................................................................................................................

.................................................................................................................................

**Internet of THINGS**

**Module 29**

**Ethics**

**For more help on this topic, see Letts GCSE Computer Science Revision Guide pages 74–75.**

**3** What are the security considerations for data storage in the 'cloud'?

Do you think these are outweighed by the convenience of this sort of storage?

Explain your answer. [6 marks]

........................................................................................................................................

........................................................................................................................................

........................................................................................................................................

........................................................................................................................................

........................................................................................................................................

........................................................................................................................................

........................................................................................................................................

**4** Explain how a social network, based in the UK, must comply with the Data Protection Act. [6 marks]

........................................................................................................................................

........................................................................................................................................

........................................................................................................................................

........................................................................................................................................

........................................................................................................................................

........................................................................................................................................

........................................................................................................................................

**For more help on this topic, see Letts GCSE Computer Science Revision Guide pages 74–75.**

**1** What is a simple 'Caesar cipher'? [1 mark]

...........................................................................................................................................................

**2** Here is an example of a Caesar cipher:

| A | B | C | D | E | F | G | H | I | J | K | L | M | N | O | P | Q | R | S | T | U | V | W | X | Y | Z |
|---|---|---|---|---|---|---|---|---|---|---|---|---|---|---|---|---|---|---|---|---|---|---|---|---|---|
| E | F | G | H | I | J | K | L | M | N | O | P | Q | R | S | T | U | V | W | X | Y | Z | A | B | C | D |

Using the Caesar cipher above, decode this message. [1 mark]
CYOA YKILQPAN OYEJYA

...........................................................................................................................................................

**3** How does hashing enhance the security of a sent message? [1 mark]

...........................................................................................................................................................

...........................................................................................................................................................

**4** What is 'plaintext'? [1 mark]

...........................................................................................................................................................

**5** Describe **two** reasons why encrypted data cannot be understood by an unauthorised
person. [2 marks]

...........................................................................................................................................................

...........................................................................................................................................................

**6** Identify **two** modern uses of online encryption. [2 marks]

1. ...............................................................................................................................................

2. ...............................................................................................................................................

**7** A familiar method of encryption is SSL. Explain what SSL is and how it works. [4 marks]

...........................................................................................................................................................

...........................................................................................................................................................

...........................................................................................................................................................

...........................................................................................................................................................

...........................................................................................................................................................

...........................................................................................................................................................

**Encryption**

**Module 30**

**For more help on this topic, see Letts GCSE Computer Science Revision Guide pages 76–77.**

## GCSE
# Computer Science

**Paper 1**                                      Time: 1 hour 30 minutes

> **For this paper you must have:**
>
> - mathematical instruments
>
> You must **not** use a calculator.

### Instructions

- Use black ink or black ball-point pen. Use pencil only for drawing.
- Answer **all** the questions.
- Answer the questions in the spaces provided.
- Answer questions that require a coded solution in whichever format you prefer, as long as your meaning is clear and unambiguous.
- You must **not** use a calculator.

### Information

- The mark for each question is shown in brackets.
- The maximum mark for this paper is 70.
- Remember to use good English and clear presentation in your answers.

Name: ................................................................................................

**1** State what 10010111 is translated from binary to decimal.  [1]

...........................................................................................................................................................

**2** State what 125 is translated from decimal to binary.  [1]

...........................................................................................................................................................

**3** Below are three types of memory. Tick the name of the type of memory used to make up for the difference of speed in function of two internal components of a computer.  [1]

ROM ☐          cache ☐          volatile ☐

**4** An early form of cipher is known as a Caesar cipher, as shown below:

| A | B | C | D | E | F | G | H | I | J | K | L | M |
|---|---|---|---|---|---|---|---|---|---|---|---|---|
| N | O | P | Q | R | S | T | U | V | W | X | Y | Z |

| N | O | P | Q | R | S | T | U | V | W | X | Y | Z |
|---|---|---|---|---|---|---|---|---|---|---|---|---|
| A | B | C | D | E | F | G | H | I | J | K | L | M |

**a)** Explain how the Caesar cipher works.  [2]

...........................................................................................................................................................

...........................................................................................................................................................

...........................................................................................................................................................

...........................................................................................................................................................

...........................................................................................................................................................

**b)** Use the Caesar cipher above to decode the following:  [3]

| P | B | Z | C | H | G | R | E | F |   | H | F | R |
|---|---|---|---|---|---|---|---|---|---|---|---|---|
|   |   |   |   |   |   |   |   |   |   |   |   |   |
| O | V | A | N | E | L |   |   |   |   |   |   |   |
|   |   |   |   |   |   |   |   |   |   |   |   |   |

**5** **a)** What is the 'client-server model'?  [1]

...........................................................................................................................................................

**b)** Explain how it aids effective data transfer across the Internet.  [2]

...........................................................................................................................................................

...........................................................................................................................................................

**6** From the options below, identify (tick) **one** reason why hexadecimal is used to represent data. [1]

Hexadecimal is quicker for the computer to interpret. ☐

Hexadecimal takes up less memory in the computer. ☐

Hexadecimal is easier for humans to read. ☐

**7** A list is made up of the following numbers:

58,34,2,4,39,54,1

Show the steps involved in sorting it using merge sort. [2]

........................................................................................................................

........................................................................................................................

........................................................................................................................

........................................................................................................................

**8** The algorithm below is designed to search for a value within a list.

```
target <- 30
list <- [2,3,5,7,30,35]
found <- false
i <- 1
WHILE i≤6
    IF list[i] = target THEN
        found<- true
    ENDIF
    i = i + 1
ENDWHILE
```

**a)** Complete the trace table for this algorithm. The number of rows does **not** relate to the number of steps. [4]

| target | found | i | list[i] |
|--------|-------|---|---------|
| 30 | false | 1 | 2 |
|  |  |  |  |
|  |  |  |  |
|  |  |  |  |
|  |  |  |  |
|  |  |  |  |
|  |  |  |  |

**b)** The algorithm is currently inefficient. One of the following lines should replace the WHILE statement above. Identify (tick) the correct replacement. [1]

WHILE found = false ☐

WHILE i<=6 OR found = false ☐

WHILE i<=6 OR found = true ☐

WHILE i<=6 AND found = false ☐

9   Below is the start of an algorithm to check when workers arrive and depart from their workplace. To make the output more user friendly, the programmer wants to make the program accept a 24-hour clock input and translate it into a 12-hour display. Complete the algorithm. **[4]**

```
OUTPUT<- "Enter the 24 hour number of arrival"
hour <-USERINPUT
```

10  A robot is controlled using an algorithm holding four subroutines:

FD (x) moves the robot x squares forward
LT (x) moves the robot x degree left
RT (x) moves the robot x degrees right
Obstacle() is a Boolean control registering TRUE if the way forward is blocked, FALSE otherwise.

a)  Draw the path of the robot if it followed these instructions. **[2]**

```
FD (3)
LT (90)
FD (3)
RT (90)
FD (1)
```

START

**b)** Write the instructions so that the robot is able to follow this path. **[2]**

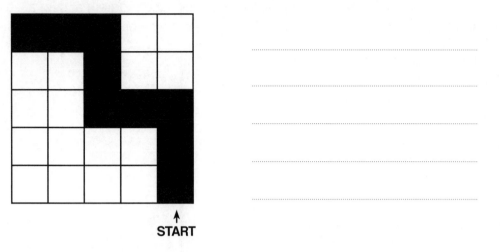

START

**11** A Huffman tree for EVERYONE HAD FUN AT THE PARTY is shown below. Complete the missing elements in the table below. **[3]**

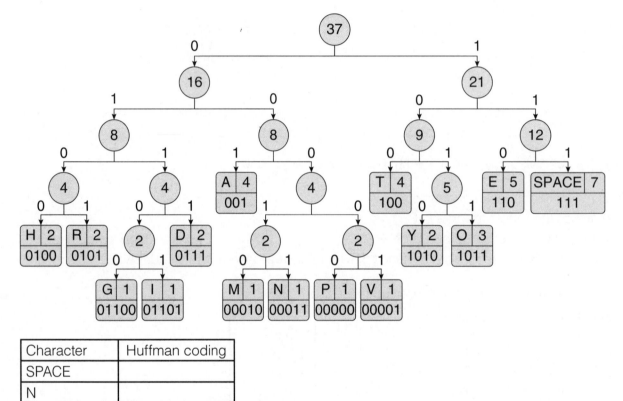

| Character | Huffman coding |
|-----------|----------------|
| SPACE     |                |
| N         |                |
| A         |                |

**12** The two tables below form a relational database.

Stock:

| StockName | Code | WarehouseLocation | Styles |
|---|---|---|---|
| T-shirt | TSH | Area45 | 2 |
| Jeans | BJE | Area12 | 7 |
| Trainers | TRA | Area09 | 1 |
| Socks | SOX | Area25 | 1 |
| Hoodie | SWH | Area40 | 4 |

Warehouse:

| WarehouseLocation | SpaceUsed | Zone |
|---|---|---|
| Area45 | 15 | A |
| Area12 | 30 | B |
| Area09 | 30 | C |
| Area25 | 8 | C |
| Area40 | 15 | A |

**a)** State one field in the Warehouse table which will be the primary key. **[1]**

**b)** State how many records there are in the Stock table. **[1]**

**c)** Explain how the relationship between the two tables has been created. **[2]**

**13** The black and white image below consists of 36 pixels.

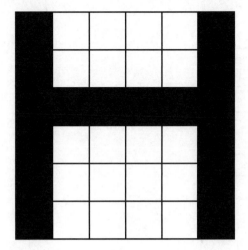

    **a)** Explain why 36 bits are required. [2]

    ................................................................................................................................................

    ................................................................................................................................................

    **b)** State how many bits would be needed if the image had four colours not two. [1]

    ................................................................................................................................................

**14** Define the term 'resolution'. [1]

................................................................................................................................................

................................................................................................................................................

**15** Explain the purpose of an operating system. [2]

................................................................................................................................................

................................................................................................................................................

**16** In binary addition, show the result of 100101 + 10101. Show your working. [2]

................................................................................................................................................

................................................................................................................................................

**17** Which of the following are common data types handled by most programming languages? Tick **two**. [2]

Maximum ☐

Character ☐

While ☐

Length ☐

Boolean ☐

**18** Show the process in bubble sorting in the dataset below. [3]

16,21,11,19

............................................................................................................................

............................................................................................................................

............................................................................................................................

............................................................................................................................

............................................................................................................................

............................................................................................................................

**19** In a bubble sort, tick the maximum number of swaps, if there are five numbers in the dataset to be sorted. [1]

2 ☐

10 ☐

25 ☐

30 ☐

**20** What is the worst-case scenario for bubble sort? Explain why. [4]

............................................................................................................................

............................................................................................................................

............................................................................................................................

............................................................................................................................

**21** Write an algorithm to calculate the average test score in a class of 10. You can use either pseudocode or a flowchart. **[4]**

**22** State the index of the value 9 in the dataset below. For the purposes of this exercise, the index starts at [1]. **[1]**

23,12,4,9,1,30,3

**23** Tick the following statements that are **true**. [1]

Arrays are of fixed size, so they cannot be edited without rewriting the code. ☐

Arrays allow only sequential access to the data they contain. ☐

Arrays can only store data of one type. ☐

**24** The following code is a function:

```
FUNCTION HelloWorld (greeting,name)
   IF greeting[1] = "Hello"
      OUTPUT true
   ELSE
      OUTPUT false
   ENDIF
ENDFUNCTION
```

**a)** State the data structure for 'greeting'. [1]

...........................................................................................................................................................

**b)** State the data type for the output value. [1]

...........................................................................................................................................................

**25** Give **two** reasons why programmers use functions. [2]

...........................................................................................................................................................

...........................................................................................................................................................

...........................................................................................................................................................

**26** What is a 'parameter'? Tick **one**. [1]

A small section of a program ☐

A value used to control a function ☐

The data sent to a function by the subroutine that called it ☐

**28** Tick the type of error that will allow the program to run, but will produce an incorrect answer. [1]

Run time error ☐

Logic error ☐

Syntax error ☐

**28** Compare the benefits of coding in high-level and low-level programming language.
Your answer should begin with a definition of each type of language. **[6]**

.......................................................................................................................................................................

.......................................................................................................................................................................

.......................................................................................................................................................................

.......................................................................................................................................................................

.......................................................................................................................................................................

.......................................................................................................................................................................

.......................................................................................................................................................................

.......................................................................................................................................................................

.......................................................................................................................................................................

.......................................................................................................................................................................

.......................................................................................................................................................................

.......................................................................................................................................................................

.......................................................................................................................................................................

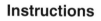

# GCSE
# Computer Science

**Paper 2**                                    Time: 1 hour 30 minutes

**For this paper you must have:**

- mathematical instruments

You must **not** use a calculator.

## Instructions

- Use black ink or black ball-point pen. Use pencil only for drawing.
- Answer **all** the questions.
- Answer the questions in the spaces provided.
- Answer questions that require a coded solution in whichever format you prefer, as long as your meaning is clear and unambiguous.
- You must **not** use a calculator.

## Information

- The mark for each question is shown in brackets.
- The maximum mark for this paper is 73.
- Remember to use good English and clear presentation in your answers.

Name:

**1** Describe the differences between a **ring** network and a **bus** network, highlighting the advantages and disadvantages of each. **[5 marks]**

.......................................................................................................................................................

.......................................................................................................................................................

.......................................................................................................................................................

.......................................................................................................................................................

.......................................................................................................................................................

**2** Explain the difference between a LAN and a WAN. Give examples of both types of network. **[4 marks]**

.......................................................................................................................................................

.......................................................................................................................................................

.......................................................................................................................................................

.......................................................................................................................................................

**3** Discuss the following statement: **[6 marks]**

"A wireless network is more convenient, but less secure, than a wired network."

.......................................................................................................................................................

.......................................................................................................................................................

.......................................................................................................................................................

.......................................................................................................................................................

.......................................................................................................................................................

.......................................................................................................................................................

4   Complete the following TCP/IP model of the Internet.         **[3 marks]**

| APPLICATION LAYER |
| :--- |
| _____ LAYER |
| _____ LAYER |
| _____ (or DATA LINK) LAYER |

5   Below there are three network protocols. Tick **one** which is solely used by email communication.  **[1 mark]**

TCP/IP  ☐

IMAP  ☐

HTML  ☐

6   Communication across a network is expressed in Mbps. Calculate how many bits are being transmitted per second for a network with a 5 Mbps connection.    **[3 marks]**

7   Complete the truth table for the following logic circuit:       **[6 marks]**

| A | B | D | K | Z |
| :---: | :---: | :---: | :---: | :---: |
| 0 | 0 | | | |
| 0 | 1 | | | |
| 1 | 0 | | | |
| 1 | 1 | | | |

**8** Boolean operators are used in embedded systems.

**a)** State what an 'embedded system' is. **[1 mark]**

.........................................................................................................................................................................

.........................................................................................................................................................................

**b)** Describe **one** function of the embedded system in a washing machine. **[1 mark]**

.........................................................................................................................................................................

.........................................................................................................................................................................

**9** Complete the truth table for the AND logic gate. **[1 mark]**

| A | B | A AND B |
|---|---|---------|
| 0 | 0 | |
| 0 | 1 | |
| 1 | 0 | |
| 1 | 1 | |

**10** A logic circuit is being developed for a lift door. The door has a sensor each side (A) and (B). The door opens when one is triggered, and can also be opened or closed using an override switch (O). The output is shown in Z. Complete the following logic circuit diagram. **[3 marks]**

A

B

Z

O

**11** A small business wants to explore storing their data in the 'cloud'. One of their team is worried about this. Explain the benefits and potential disadvantages of storing data in the cloud. Your answer should include a clear definition of the 'cloud'. **[6 marks]**

.........................................................................................................................................................................

.........................................................................................................................................................................

.........................................................................................................................................................................

.........................................................................................................................................................................

.........................................................................................................................................................................

.........................................................................................................................................................................

**12** Many people resist using files such as MP3 and JPG for their multimedia files. Explain why this might be. **[2 marks]**

...................................................................................................................................................................................................

**13** Tick the following statement that is **true** about run length encoding. **[1 mark]**

It is most effective on images with many continuous pixels of the same colour ☐

It is most effective on photographs ☐

It produces a lossy format ☐

**14** One method of data compression is Huffman coding. Here are three types of data. Tick the type that is compressed using Huffman coding. **[1 mark]**

Text data ☐

Graphical data ☐

Sound data ☐

**15** Operating systems are an example of which type of software? Tick **one**. **[1 mark]**

Application software ☐

System software ☐

**16** Describe what a 'high-level' programming language is. Explain why this is preferred by programmers for some tasks. **[3 marks]**

...................................................................................................................................................................................................

...................................................................................................................................................................................................

...................................................................................................................................................................................................

...................................................................................................................................................................................................

**17** "Subroutines make the process of algorithm writing easier". Discuss this statement. **[6 marks]**

...................................................................................................................................................................................................

...................................................................................................................................................................................................

...................................................................................................................................................................................................

...................................................................................................................................................................................................

...................................................................................................................................................................................................

...................................................................................................................................................................................................

**18** A patch for an email application is available. Explain why users should always apply patches for software. **[2 marks]**

.....................................................................................................................................................

.....................................................................................................................................................

**19** What is a data structure? Tick **one**. **[1 mark]**

A way of organising data so that it can be used efficiently ☐

A way of organising data so that it is neater ☐

A way of organising data so that it is easy to input ☐

**20** Computer systems now manage critical data across our lives. Discuss **two** ways in which we can help ensure the safety and security of this data, whether at home, in school or at work. **[6 marks]**

.....................................................................................................................................................

.....................................................................................................................................................

.....................................................................................................................................................

.....................................................................................................................................................

.....................................................................................................................................................

.....................................................................................................................................................

.....................................................................................................................................................

.....................................................................................................................................................

.....................................................................................................................................................

.....................................................................................................................................................

**21 a)** State what 'data validation' is. **[1 mark]**

.....................................................................................................................................................

.....................................................................................................................................................

**b)** Identify **two** methods of validation. **[2 marks]**

.....................................................................................................................................................

.....................................................................................................................................................

.....................................................................................................................................................

22 The statements below are about variables. Tick the statement which is **true**. **[1 mark]**

A variable is data stored in memory that can be changed. ☐

A variable is data stored in memory that cannot be changed. ☐

A variable is created by the computer. ☐

23 A software entry screen requires a UK mobile phone number to be entered.
Describe the **three** types of test data that can be used and give examples of each. **[6 marks]**

# ASCII table

| Character | Decimal number | Binary number | Character | Decimal number | Binary number |
|---|---|---|---|---|---|
| blank space | 32 | 0010 0000 | ^ | 94 | 0101 1110 |
| ! | 33 | 0010 0001 | - | 95 | 0101 1111 |
| " | 34 | 0010 0010 | ' | 96 | 0110 0000 |
| # | 35 | 0010 0011 | a | 97 | 0110 0001 |
| $ | 36 | 0010 0100 | b | 98 | 0110 0010 |
| A | 65 | 0100 0001 | c | 99 | 0110 0011 |
| B | 66 | 0100 0010 | d | 100 | 0110 0100 |
| C | 67 | 0100 0011 | e | 101 | 0110 0101 |
| D | 68 | 0100 0100 | f | 102 | 0110 0110 |
| E | 69 | 0100 0101 | g | 103 | 0110 0111 |
| F | 70 | 0100 0110 | h | 104 | 0110 1000 |
| G | 71 | 0100 0111 | i | 105 | 0110 1001 |
| H | 72 | 0100 1000 | j | 106 | 0110 1010 |
| I | 73 | 0100 1001 | k | 107 | 0110 1011 |
| J | 74 | 0100 1010 | l | 108 | 0110 1100 |
| K | 75 | 0100 1011 | m | 109 | 0110 1101 |
| L | 76 | 0100 1100 | n | 110 | 0110 1110 |
| M | 77 | 0100 1101 | o | 111 | 0110 1111 |
| N | 78 | 0100 1110 | p | 112 | 0111 0000 |
| O | 79 | 0100 1111 | q | 113 | 0111 0001 |
| P | 80 | 0101 0000 | r | 114 | 0111 0010 |
| Q | 81 | 0101 0001 | s | 115 | 0111 0011 |
| R | 82 | 0101 0010 | t | 116 | 0111 0100 |
| S | 83 | 0101 0011 | u | 117 | 0111 0101 |
| T | 84 | 0101 0100 | v | 118 | 0111 0110 |
| U | 85 | 0101 0101 | w | 119 | 0111 0111 |
| V | 86 | 0101 0110 | x | 120 | 0111 1000 |
| W | 87 | 0101 0111 | y | 121 | 0111 1001 |
| X | 88 | 0101 1000 | z | 122 | 0111 1010 |

# Answers

## Module 1: Representing algorithms
1. An algorithm is a sequence of steps **(1)** that can be followed to complete a task **(1)**.
2. This flowchart outputs 'counting' **(1)**, then counts sequentially by 1s up to 5 **(1)** and outputs 'done' **(1)**.
3.

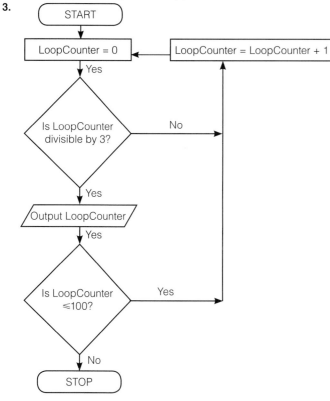

**[5 marks: 1 mark for structure, 1 mark for each shape within the start/stop endings]**

4. The amount of resources it uses in one complete cycle **(1)**.
   The time it takes to complete one complete cycle **(1)**.
5. Select Program
   Select File and Open
   Enter Password
   Edit Data
   Save and Close
   **[5 marks: 1 mark for each entry correctly placed]**
6. Iteration is repetition of a process **(1)**.
7. Breaking a problem into sub-problems **(1)**, each of which is a task on its own **(1)**.
8. Abstraction is the process of removing unnecessary details **(1)** from a problem or task such that a computer can process the task **(1)**.
9. A trace table works through the program line by line **(1)** to track the variables as they change through the program **(1)**.

## Module 2: Searching algorithms
1. Calculate mid-point
   Compare value to mid-point
   If >, perform binary search on the left sub-list
   If <, perform binary search on the right sub-list **[4 marks: 1 mark for each step]**.
2. A linear search works by looking at every item or set of data in turn **(1)** until the details that you are searching for are found (or you fail to find it altogether) **(1)**.
3. Linear search **(1)** – you can see this because it goes from the first item in the array.
4. It is called brute force searching because it goes through each item without prioritising them, one by one, until it reaches the data sought **(1)**.

5. It starts its search at the middle value **(1)**, then splits the dataset **(1)** according to whether the data sought is above or below the middle value **(1)**.
6. If the data is unsorted **(1)** or the value is near the start of the file **(1)**.
7. Binary search **(1)** because the dataset is sorted **(1)**.
8. Linear search **(1)** because the list is fairly small and not sorted **(1)**.

## Module 3: Sorting algorithms
1. A ✓ **(1)**
2. (6,2,4,1,8) to (2,6,4,1,8)
   (2,6,4,1,8) to (2,4,6,1,8)
   (2,4,6,1,8) to (2,4,1,6,8)
   (2,4,1,6,8) to (2,1,4,6,8)
   (2,1,4,6,8) to (1,2,4,6,8)
   Total five steps
   **[4 marks: 1 mark for correct method, 2 marks for correct sequence, 1 mark for correct number of steps stated]**
3.

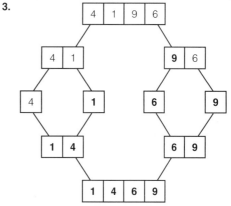

**[3 marks: 1 mark for correct split, 1 mark for correct merge, 1 mark for correct answer]**

## Module 4: Data types
1. A Boolean data type has one of two values, generally identified as 'true' and 'false', or '1' and '0' **(1)**.
2. A telephone number would be a string **(1)** because it is used as an identifier **(1)** and is not used as a basis for any calculations **(1)**.
3. In computer science a variable is a location in memory **(1)** used to store data, it has an identifier **(1)**. The value within this location can change as a result of the processes operated by the program **(1)**.
4. 5 **(1)**
5. When you declare a constant you also give it a value at the point of declaration **(1)**; constants cannot be modified or assigned a new value without rewriting the code **(1)**. An example would be DaysInYear = 365. When you declare a variable, you are uniquely identifying **(1)** a space in memory that will hold a value **(1)** that can be manipulated by code. An example would be HoursWorked = input("Hours worked this week: ")
6. Iteration **(1)**; also known as repeating a set of instructions a number of times.
7. Iteration allows the programmer to code one sequence of steps to be run through a set number of times **(1)** to achieve a required outcome, without having to write that set of steps repeatedly **(1)**. This keeps code shorter **(1)** and makes it easier to test **(1)**. You may not know how many times code has to run, so cannot physically write it.

## Module 5: Pseudocode
1. Pseudocode is an informal set of programming language style instructions for an algorithm or program **(1)** that is designed to be easily read and doesn't use any specific syntax **(1)**.

2. 
```
Input student mark
If student mark > 30
    print 'passed'
Else (1)
    print 'did not pass'
End (1)
```
3. Counts **(1)** and prints **(1)** numbers up to 100 **(1)**.
4. Prints all numbers between a user-set start and finish point **(1)**, printing an error message **(1)** if the start number is larger than the finish number **(1)**.
5. 
```
Input Number1
Input Number2
Input Number3 (1)
Sum = Number1+Number2+Number3
print "The sum of the numbers is: " + "Sum (1)
Product = Number1*Number2*Number3"
print "The product of the numbers is: " +
"Product" (1)
```

## Module 6: Arithmetic, relational and Boolean operators in programming languages

1. 
```
Input a
input b
c = a*b
print c (1)
```
2. Code 1 would show the integer value of 13/2, which is 7 **(1)**. Code 2 would show the 'real' or 'float' value, which is 6.5 **(1)**. The integer value is the rounded up whole number result of the calculation **(1)**.
3. Because you cannot use mathematical operators on strings like 'Name': you can only use mathematical operators on numbers **(1)**.
4. The coder used division (/) on the calculation of pay based on hours worked and pay rate **(1)**. This should have been a * for multiplication **(1)**.
5. Although b has a value lower than 50, a is greater than 10 **(1)**, so the printout would be 'Extra Homework!' **(1)**.
6. b still has the lower value, but now the code is looking for a being equal to or greater than 10 **(1)**. So now the display shows "Class Dismissed!" **(1)**.

## Module 7: Flowcharts

1. a = decision **(1)**
   b = terminator (START/STOP) **(1)**
   c = input/output **(1)**
   d = process **(1)**
2. When an input value is entered, the flowchart checks if it is greater than or equal to 10 **(1)**. If it is not, the "Outside acceptable range" statement is given and resets **(1)**. If it is, the flowchart checks if it is also equal to or less than 20 **(1)**. If not, it resets again and if it is, the final "Acceptable range" message is given and the flowchart stops **(1)**.
3. 

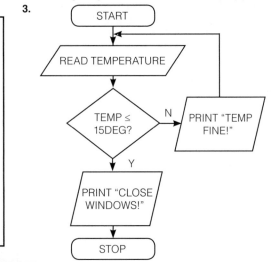

## Module 8: Data structures

1. 

| 1 | 1 | 1 | 1 |
|---|---|---|---|
| 1 | 0 | 0 | 0 |
| 1 | 0 | 0 | 0 |
| 1 | 1 | 1 | 1 |

**(2)**

2. Data structures define how data is formatted and stored **(1)** to allow for efficient search, retrieval and processing **(1)**.
3. Output would be "pears" **(1)** because all lists are indexed starting at 0 **(1)**.
4. No **(1)** because arrays do not accept mixed data types **(1)**.
5. The array has 6x6 elements **(1)** – 36 in total **(1)**.
6. 6 is the 5th item **(1)** because all indexes start at 0.
7. An array is static in that its size is fixed and cannot be updated **(1)**.

## Module 9: Input/output and file handling

1. It would open a csv file **(1)** called contacts **(1)**. It then asks the user to input their name and phone number **(1)** and then saves the new data to the file **(1)**.
2. External sensors **(1)**, e.g. temperature, movement or sound. User input **(1)**, e.g. keyboard, mouse, touchscreen.
3. An index allows the computer to search the database more effectively **(1)**, because it is possible to search the index **(1)** rather than the whole database to locate the element sought.
4. Because the computer cannot check if you are telling the truth **(1)** – only that the data you enter is within the limits that have been set **(1)**.
5. 
```
file = open("classlist.csv", "a")
name (1) = input("Please enter name.")
file.write (1) (name + ","+ "\n")
```
6. The file would be overwritten everyday, meaning older versions could not be accessed **(1)**. A solution would be to create a daily backup with an alternative filename **(1)**.

## Module 10: String handling

1. A string data type can contain any alphanumeric character **(1)**, including punctuation **(1)**.
2. 

| Data type | Store as an integer | Store as a string |
|---|---|---|
| Steve | | ✓ |
| 15 | ✓ | |
| 007 | | ✓ |
| 2010 | ✓ | |
| 10.2 | | ✓ |
| 01501 2987659 | | ✓ |

**[4 marks if fully correct, 3 marks if four correct, 2 marks if three correct, 1 mark if one correct]**

3. "fishchipsmushy peas" **(1)** because there is no clear space set up between the strings **(1)**.
4. 102 **(1)**
5. So that the computer can distinguish between the two possible data entries, as in passwords, for example **(1)**.

## Module 11: Random number generation in a programming language

1. A random number is generated by a process with an outcome that cannot be predicted or reproduced **(1)**. A pseudorandom number is a computer-generated random number that appears to have the same properties but is created using statistical patterns that can be repeated and therefore it is not truly random **(1)**.

(2)

Answers

2. Any two from: user ID generation; online gambling; computer games; online password generators; cryptography services.
**[2 marks: 1 mark for each use]**
3. It chooses a random integer **(1)** of value between 1 and 100 **(1)**, and encourages the users to guess the number. It counts the number of guesses and outputs that number as part of the message **(1)** when the user gets the number right. The random function in this code ensures that truly no one knows in advance the value of the number to be guessed **(1)**.

## Module 12: Databases
1. A flat-file database has only one table **(1)**, such as an Excel worksheet which shows the prices of products in a store **(1)**. A relational database has several different tables linked together **(1)**, such as a school database that contains details of students, staff, classes **(1)**.
2. A primary key is a data entry uniquely identified to each record within the database **(1)**.
3. Structured data is data organised into a specific format **(1)**, such as your contacts on your phone **(1)**. Unstructured data is like a list of your IMs or the contents of your social media photo account **(1)**: there is no coherent organisation **(1)**.
4. To output the data in a way that is easy for humans to read **(1)**.
5. (a)

| D | 335948 | Shirt | White | M | £12.99 | **(1)** |
|---|--------|-------|-------|---|--------|---------|

(b)

| D | 335948 | Shirt | White | M | £12.99 |
|---|--------|-------|-------|---|--------|
| F | 222687 | Shirt | Blue | M | £12.99 |

**[2 marks: 1 mark for each correct row]**

(c)

| A | 569875 | T-shirt | Blue | S | £14.99 |
|---|--------|---------|------|---|--------|
| D | 335948 | Shirt | White | M | £12.99 |
| E | 798994 | Socks | White | 5 | £6.99 |
| F | 222687 | Shirt | Blue | M | £12.99 |

**[4 marks: 1 mark for each correct row]**

## Module 13: Introduction to subroutines and structured programming
1. Any three from: clearly breaking a big task into little ones makes the big task more achievable; using self-contained code modules or subroutines (one for each part of the task) makes it easy to see which part of the code does which part of the overall task; updates are a lot easier – you just change the bit that needs to be updated; can be called from the main program, or another subroutine.
**[3 marks: 1 mark for each correct example]**
2. A comment is an annotation of the code only relevant to the human reader – the computer overlooks it. It helps the human reader see what is supposed to happen, and is identified using a convention **(1)** such as #Total The Amount in this section **(1)**.
3. Assembler **(1)**: A program that translates assembly language into machine code **(1)**.
Compiler **(1)**: A program that translates high-level programmer written code into low-level machine code **(1)**.
Interpreter **(1)**: A program that translates programmer code line by line **(1)** into machine code.
4. 1. Comments in the code **(1)**
   2. Clear variable names **(1)**
   3. Modules and functions appropriately named **(1)**
   4. Use indented code where available **(1)**

## Module 14: Parameters and subroutines
1. Any one from: name; value **(1)**.
2. Any two from: the code can be written once, then used more than once, as needed, such as a greenhouse temperature monitoring system; keeps code shorter because you are only writing the code once for the subroutine, no matter how many times you need it, your code overall can be considerably shorter; easier to test even large tasks, if decomposed into smaller subtasks, can be easy to test one module – or subroutine – at a time; you can access and use any variable from your main code without having to redefine it.
**[2 marks: 1 mark for each example]**
3. Accept an answer such as:
```
Sub ImageCheck (1)
maxFileSize = 1 (1)
input "file to be uploaded" (1)
Check file properties (1)
IF filesize <= max
     UPLOAD file
ELSE
     output "file too large" (1)
ENDIF
EndSub (1)
```
4. (a)

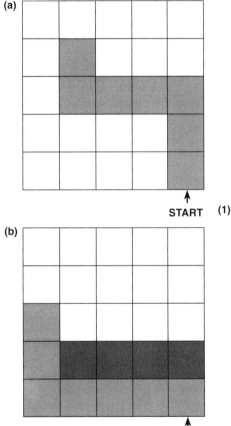

START **(1)**

(b)

START **(1)**

(c) Accept answers such as:
FD (1)
LT (90)
FD (3)
RT (90)
FD (4)
RT (90)
FD (3) **(1)**

### Module 15: Robust and secure programming

1. Validation ensures that the data is within reasonable limits **(1)**, such as a date of birth, or a postcode **(1)**. It does not test whether the data is actually true **(1)**.

    Verification checks whether the data is true **(1)**, and this is generally a human task **(1)** rather than a computer one. Date of birth, for example, can be confirmed with a birth certificate or driver's licence or passport **(1)**.

2. Accept answers such as:

    Make some answers 'required' so that they can rank against them.

    Ask for the same information in different ways so that if the answers differ then something isn't right.

    **[2 marks: 1 mark for method, 1 mark for description]**

3. Accept answers such as:

    TimeIn >= 0700 AND TimeIn < 1200. 'nine o'clock' would be invalid.

    **[2 marks if fully correct, 1 mark for valid time control]**

4. Any two from: making sure the program runs without errors; testing confirms that the product that has been created to meet the original specification criteria or problem; mimicking user input with different data to make sure all possible values are dealt with appropriately; eliminating the need to withdraw and re-release a program.

    **[2 marks: 1 mark for each point made]**

5. Normal: e.g. 01/10/1974 **(1)**

    Extreme: 01/01/2000 or 31/12/1999 **(1)**

    Erroneous: e.g. 5th June 1969 **(1)**

### Module 16: Number bases and binary arithmetic

1. It is easier to translate into decimal **(1)**, easier to understand **(1)**. Each hexadecimal digit represents 4 bits, or a nibble, so two hexadecimal digits represent a byte **(1)**.

2. A = 10 * 16, 2 = 2

    160 + 2 = 162 **[2 marks: 1 mark for correct working, 1 mark for correct answer]**

3. 
    ```
      00000111
    + 00000111
      00001110
    ```
    **[2 marks: 1 mark for correct working, 1 mark for correct answer]**

4. 
    $16^2$  $16^1$  $16^0$

    = 256   16   1

    ≈ 1   0   0

    = 100

    **[2 marks: 1 mark for correct working, 1 mark for correct answer]**

### Module 17: Units of information and character encoding

1. **(a)** 8 **(1)**

    **(b)** 256 **(1)**

    **(c)** 2048 **(1)**

2. Any one from: 1 coded as black and 0 as white; 1 as white and 0 as black **(1)**.

3. A nibble **(1)**

4. A gigabyte (GB) is 1024 megabytes **(1)**.

    A terabyte (TB) is 1024 gigabytes **(1)**.

5. There are 16 possible binary numbers **(1)**, so 16 possible codes may be actioned **(1)**.

6. 256 colours **(1)**

7. Colour depth is used to describe the maximum number of colours that could be used in the graphic **(1)**. The higher the number of colours then the more complex the colour palette – and the larger the file size **(1)**.

8. The original 128 characters within ASCII are not sufficient to represent all of the possible characters, numbers and symbols in languages across the world **(1)**. Unicode includes the non-Western languages that ASCII doesn't recognise or accommodate **(1)**. Unicode has separate character sets for the majority of written languages across the globe.

### Module 18: Representing images and sound

1. The program takes a number of samples of the sound at regular set intervals **(1)**, and works out the 'top' and 'bottom' values of the analogue sound within each sample **(1)**. If the sound being processed is 'above' the halfway point, the program checks again if the sound would still be above halfway if the first half was cut into half again, and so on. 'Above' is recorded as a '1', 'below' it is recorded as a '0' **(1)**. The more samples per second that are taken, the higher the quality of sound – and the larger the file **(1)**.

2. Bit depth is the number of bits available for each sample taken from the sound **(1)**. The greater the bit depth, the better the quality of sound **(1)**.

3. MP3 is a lossy compression format so a lot of data is lost in the compression, thus reducing the size.

    **or**

    WAV is a lossless compression format so very little data is lost in compression, meaning that the file size isn't reduced as substantially.

    **[2 marks: 1 mark for description, 1 mark for explanation]**

4. Resolution refers to how many pixels are used per square **(1)**. Low-resolution graphics are coarser **(1)** and may seem 'furry'; high resolution graphics have more pixels per square **(1)** and therefore are clearer and sharper **(1)**.

5. JPEGs allow compression of graphics in a lossy format, meaning that data quality is lost **(1)** as the file is increasingly compressed **(1)**, but JPEGs can also be saved in full uncompressed detail **(1)**.

6. A pixel is short for Picture Element, and is a single 'dot' on your screen or printout **(1)**. It is a square of one colour used to make a bitmap image **(1)**.

### Module 19: Data compression

1. A Huffman tree shows the frequency of elements in a file, coding the most frequent ones with the smallest number **(1)**, to limit the file size overall in a lossless compression strategy **(1)**.

2. RLE is a very simple form of lossless data compression **(1)** which converts consecutive identical elements by storing the number of identical elements as a code **(1)**.

3. When it is used on images that have many continuous identical colour pixels black and white image, for example **(1)**.

4. 
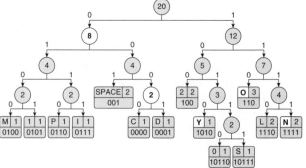

**[5 marks: 1 mark for each correct element]**

### Module 20: Hardware, software and Boolean logic

1. Any two from: defragmentation software moves file blocks closer together; so that the computer can load files more quickly; compression software reduces file sizes using less space so that the files may be loaded more quickly; some type of backup software could be used to move files to a secure place, then the user could delete the less often used

files on the hard disc to free up space; which would improve the speed of the disc. **[2 marks: 1 mark for each correct example]**

2. Bus ✓ **(1)**

3. Hardware is the collective name given to the physical (or electrical) components (or parts) of a computer system **(1)**.

4. RAM memory is the workspace of the computer. If there isn't enough capacity in memory for the CPU needs, the computer has to set up what's known as a virtual memory file **(1)**. To do this the CPU reserves space on the hard disk to simulate (or pretend to be) additional RAM. This process, referred to as 'swapping', slows the system down **(1)**.

5.

| A | B | A OR B |
|---|---|--------|
| 0 | 0 | **0** |
| 0 | 1 | **1** |
| 1 | 0 | **1** |
| 1 | 1 | **1** |

**[2 marks if fully correct, 1 mark for the first two lines]**

6. Two colours are needed so only two possible bit patterns – which can be represented with one bit showing either 0 or 1 **(1)**: therefore 25 pixels will need 25 bits **(1)**.

## Module 21: Software classification

1. Any one from: word processing; spreadsheet; desktop publishing **(1)**. It is not enough to simply name a product like 'Keynote' or 'Word'.

2. Anti-virus checker ✓ **(1)**

3. Open source software is provided with a licence that means it can be downloaded, along with its source code, used, edited or redistributed for any purpose **(1)**.

4. A Command Line Interface is the text based way of communicating with the computer **(1)**. It is not particularly efficient nor is it user friendly **(1)**. A Graphical User Interface is the basis of most systems today, like iOS, WindowsX and MacOSx, where icons replace the words **(1)** and a mouse is used more than a keyboard **(1)**.

5. The OS is needed to provide an interface between application software/user and hardware **(1)** and to handle input/output devices **(1)**. It is responsible for memory management **(1)** and for allocating processor time **(1)**. It also provides security **(1)**.

6. A device driver is a small program or software interface **(1)** that enables an operating system to communicate with a hardware device **(1)** such as a printer or graphics card.

## Module 22: Systems architecture

1. Volatile memory (such as Read Access Memory) **(1)** will only hold data in memory as long as there is a power source, whereas non-volatile memory (such as USB storage) **(1)** will keep contents when power is disconnected **(1)**.

2. A Von Neumann bottleneck occurs when an 'instruction fetch' and 'data operation' cannot occur at the same time because they use the same bus **(1)**.

3. The fetch-execute cycle is the process by which the CPU reads (fetches) instructions from the memory cache, decodes them, and then operates – or executes – the instruction **(1)**.

4. RAM loses its content when the power is switched off **(1)** and ROM is read-only so cannot be edited **(1)**.

5. Level 1 cache ✓ **(1)**

6. Virtual memory is a section of the hard drive that is used when the computer does not have access to enough RAM to complete the tasks in the program **(1)**.

7. The computer uses cache memory as a form of buffer because the CPU works faster than RAM **(1)**. The data is pushed into cache memory before the CPU needs it to stop the slower memory inhibiting the function of the CPU **(1)**.

8. Buses are wires around the motherboard that connect the components that are attached **(1)**.

9. The number of cores **(1)** and the cache memory **(1)**.

## Module 23: Secondary storage

1. Optical **(1)**. CD/DVD/Blu-ray **(1)**

2. A '–R' disc can only be written to once **(1)** whereas a '–RW' disc can be erased and re-written multiple times **(1)**.

3. You can come to either conclusion – that cloud storage is a good or not-so-good option for the organisation. Your comments should include elements such as:

| Advantages of cloud storage | Disadvantages of cloud storage |
|---|---|
| Access from anywhere with Internet connection. So if they have travelling representatives they can access files and update diaries, for example. | You need a reliable Internet connection – especially if you are handling large files. So if they have travelling representatives they might be trying to access diaries or online files and find that they cannot. |
| For businesses, this means that offices across the world can access the same files. | You are relying on someone else to keep your files safe. |
| Disaster recovery is easier – assuming that your storage provider wasn't affected by whatever hit your system. So if the organisation is holding staff and customer data it is easier to recover without imposing on the people. | Moving from one provider to another can be difficult. So you need to be sure that they meet the standards you need as a small organisation. |
| Costs are generally lower per MB and storage capacity is more flexible than local storage. So this can be a better idea for a small organisation that is balancing costs carefully. | There can be data ownership issues if your provider is sold to another company – when Facebook bought Instagram, all Instagram content transferred a 'licence to use' that content to Facebook – without users' express consent. So the data they hold might well be given away to a bigger company, breaking the law. They need to be sure that this is not going to happen. |

**[8 marks: 0–2 marks – A poor response containing little explanation of advantages and disadvantages. No use of technical language and poor use of spelling and grammar; 3–5 marks – A response is given that relates to the scenario. Some advantages and disadvantages are given with some explanation. Some examples are provided and there is some use of technical language. Only minor errors in spelling and grammar; 6–8 marks – A detailed response is given that is related to the scenario. Advantages and disadvantages are given and explained fully. There is a balanced discussion and all examples are relevant and appropriate. There are few, if any, errors in spelling and grammar.]**

4. An embedded system is one in which the computer system plays a part in a much bigger device. The computer element is often nearly invisible, but essential **(1)**. Examples include digital watches/MP3 players/traffic lights **(1)**.

5. Any two from: solid state media can be more compact than magnetic media: the smaller size enables better portability; the battery will last longer because solid state media uses less power; speed of access is higher in solid state drives so you can more quickly access your data; solid state is silent, so it can be used in a wider variety of settings.
**[4 marks: 2 marks for each reason]**

## Module 24: Definitions and types of networks

1. A network often based on Bluetooth connection between devices such as keyboards, pointing devices, phones, audio headsets and printers **(1)**. These cover very short distances (up to about 10 metres) but have the advantage that they can move with the user **(1)**.

2. A LAN is a network in which all connected devices are relatively close together, in a single building or premises **(1)** like a school or office complex **(1)**. A WAN is a network in which the connected devices are too thinly spread to make a physical connection **(1)** and is used by multinational organisations and even the Internet could be described as a WAN **(1)**.

3. Wireless **(1)**. Suitable if they use their laptops in a portable manner (e.g. hot desking) **(1)**, if they all work in a relatively small area and can rely on appropriate WAP points **(1)**, if their network connection is secure (i.e. password protected) **(1)** and if there isn't a lot of heavy traffic (e.g. video streaming) across the network **(1)**.

4. You can argue for either point of view, just make sure you include evidence such as:
   Allowing wireless connectivity means:
   - it allows students to make use of their own portable devices in their learning;
   - maintaining a safe learning environment is very important as students are more vulnerable to safety issues (like trailing wires);
   - it allows computing devices to be used outside of the lesson, e.g. in PE or drama;
   - schools have limited budgets and it is cheaper to add extra wireless devices to a school network;
   - less cable and drilling are needed when expanding the network and this may save money;
   - there are now many devices which don't have wired connection ports and schools/students may want to be able to use these devices.
   And barring wireless connectivity means:
   - wired networks can provide high bandwidth for when students make use of a lot of multimedia;
   - schools need high bandwidth / reliable systems as delays in lessons are not acceptable;
   - there is better security on wired networks, making it easier for schools to control/monitor how students are using the network;
   - network performance may be poor if there are large numbers of student-owned devices using the school network at any one time.

   **[8 marks: 0–2 marks – A poor response containing little justification for the argument. No use of technical language and poor use of spelling and grammar; 3–5 marks – A response is given that relates to the scenario. Some justification for the argument. Some examples are provided and there is some use of technical language. Only minor errors in spelling and grammar; 6–8 marks – A detailed response is given that is related to the scenario. Detailed justification for the argument. There is a balanced discussion and all examples are relevant and appropriate. There are few, if any, errors in spelling and grammar.]**

## Module 25: Network topology

1. A star network topology has one connection to each of the resources or devices on it **(1)**, while a mesh network connects every device to every other device **(1)**. While the mesh network is more robust **(1)**, it is also a lot more expensive. **(1)**

2. Example answer:

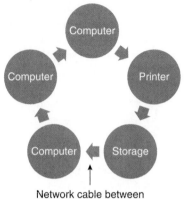

Network cable between each component

**[5 marks: 1 mark per element. Must include network cable and clear indication of the comms between devices and the ID of the devices]**

3. Each device has its own MAC address **(1)**. If the firewall has a list of those authorised to use the network resources, the MAC address of a new device can be checked against that whitelist **(1)**: if it isn't there the network is sealed against that device **(1)**.

4. A whitelist identifies authorised sites if on an Internet filter, or users or machines if on a firewall. Only those on the whitelist are allowed through. A blacklist bars only those devices or addresses identified on the list **(1)**. A whitelist is more secure **(1)**, but a blacklist is more flexible **(1)**, since the whitelist provides an absolute and limited list of devices or sites which are allowed, while the blacklist just blocks the resources or sites identified **(1)**.

5. Each packet of data has to travel through all of the devices between its origin and its destination **(1)**. If one device malfunctions the whole network is compromised **(1)**.

## Module 26: Communication protocols

1.

| APPLICATION LAYER |
| --- |
| TRANSPORT LAYER |
| INTERNET LAYER |
| NETWORK ACCESS (or DATA LINK) LAYER |

**[4 marks: 1 mark for each layer]**

2. The Transport Layer sets up the communication between the sender and the destination, making sure they agree the 'language' and also that the recipient knows the size and number of packets that it should expect **(1)**. If any go astray the Transport Layer automatically tries a number of times to re-send before transmitting a 'failed' message to the original sender so that they know the message went astray **(1)**.

3. Protocols are a set of communication standards **(1)** that govern transfer of data between devices **(1)**.

**4.**

| Action | CLIENT | SERVER | BOTH |
|---|---|---|---|
| Starting handshake | ✓ | | |
| Displaying HTML pages | ✓ | | |
| Receiving messages | | | ✓ |

**[3 marks: 1 mark for each tick]**

5. This model spreads the workload between the main server and the user's device **(1)**: a client device may share resources with the more powerful server, which enables faster communication because the server does the work before transmission **(1)**.

6. The application layer is the top-most layer and it includes protocols like DNS, HTTP(s), SMTP, IMAP, SSH, FTP **(1)**. This controls how applications access data and communicate **(1)**.

## Module 27: Definition, purpose and threat

1. A Trojan horse is a malicious computer program **(1)** that appears to the user to be of legitimate use but actually causes damage to the computer it is installed on **(1)**.

2. Accept answers such as:
   Uses a range of characters, ideally including punctuation.
   More than 8 characters long.
   Not based on a word.
   Not based on any easily known personal information (pet name, post code…).
   Easily remembered so not written down.
   Regularly (and frequently) changed.
   Not used more than once.
   **[4 marks: 1 mark for each example]**

3. Emails can be intercepted **(1)** so should never include sensitive material **(1)**. It might not be you asking for the password information **(1)**, so this might be unauthorised access **(1)**.

4. Adware is advertisements which are included in the software program and are displayed at intervals during use **(1)**. Could be dangerous, you don't know what is included, or who has built it, and it may include cookies and/or spyware **(1)**.

5. Any three from: fraudulently obtaining information by claiming to be a reputable organisation; pretending to be a bank and requesting login details; emailing a user to update personal details via a false website; creating false versions of existing websites. **[3 marks: 1 mark for each point made]**

6. Social engineering attempts to trick a user into revealing their password **(1)** and other security information through ruses such as pretending to be a new employee, or a colleague from another branch, or someone begging you for help **(1)**. Humans generally want to trust other humans, and since most of the time the request is genuine this is a hard one to beat. Asking to contact them back on an organisation phone extension can be one method of defence **(1)**, since email addresses can easily be faked **(1)**.

7. Malware can deliberately encrypt data, delete or corrupt data, destroy hard drives **(1)**, and generally cause considerable harm and distress **(1)**.

8. To control the access different users have to information ✓ **(1)**

9. This is when a site is attacked by a number of systems causing the server to shut down access to legitimate users or even entirely shut down **(1)**. A strategy for the attacker is to compromise one computer and take over its access to the Internet, then use it to infect others with malware that allows them to be controlled also **(1)**. A computer under the control of an attacker is known as a 'zombie' or 'bot' **(1)**, and botnets (collections of these hijacked computers) are often considered one of the biggest current threats to Internet security **(1)**.

10. Allowing accounts to remain of people who have left the organisation, or allowing anyone to self-register, means that the network is open to any type of abuse **(1)** – witting or unwitting. No one who does not have the right to access should have that access. No one should have more access to network resources than they absolutely need **(1)**.

11. Browser and operating system, driver and application software, are regularly updated **(1)** to ensure robustness and security **(1)** – and malware writers are constantly benefitting from those who delay their updating **(1)**. A loophole/error/back entrance may have been found that puts the computer at risk **(1)**.

## Module 28: Detecting and preventing threats

1. Encryption is the process of changing information or data **(1)** into a form that may only be understood by a recipient who has the key to decrypt it **(1)**.

2. Encoding is a way of changing information into data that the computer can process **(1)** such as changing 'Male or Female' into 'M or F' **(1)**.
   Encryption on the other hand makes the message impossible to understand by anyone who does not have the key **(1)** such as the enigma machine in WWII **(1)**.

3. 1. Online communication of personal data has to be encrypted to be safe.
   2. Governments use online secure data to transmit messages to outlying offices and embassies.
   3. Online commerce needs customers to be able to securely transmit payment details.
   4. Online banking requires that account holders can access their accounts safely.
   **[4 marks: 1 mark for each reason]**

4. Secure **(1)**

5. A private key is a very small code **(1)** used by anyone to encrypt messages **(1)** intended for a particular recipient, ensuring that the encrypted messages can be decrypted only by using a second key **(1)** that is known only to the recipient **(1)**.

6. While a 'white box' penetration test simulates an attack **(1)** by a malicious insider who knows something of the computer system under attack **(1)**, a 'black box' test simulates external hacking **(1)** or cyber warfare **(1)**.

7. Advantages – any two from: cheapest security system of all; if frequently changed, passwords can be among the most secure access devices; no specialist hardware required.
   Disadvantages – any two from: people forget them; vulnerable to brute force attacks and keyloggers; depend on users using a secure combination – and only once for each login. **[4 marks: 2 marks for two advantages, 2 marks for two disadvantages]**

8. CAPTCHA is supposed to identify human access to the site **(1)** as opposed to automated computer access **(1)**.

9. Any two from: can be difficult to read – especially for people with visual impairments; some browsers don't render them accurately ; not popular with users; audio version isn't always clear enough to understand; requires a keyboard so not entirely user friendly.
   **[2 marks: 1 mark for each disadvantage]**

10. **(a)** This is a term used in computer security to refer to the use of physical characteristics **(1)** which are unique to each person as a password or security element **(1)**, such as fingerprints or retinal scans **(1)**.
    **(b)** Passwords are often forgotten **(1)**.
    Passwords are often easily hacked **(1)**.
    Biometrics are unique to each person **(1)**.
    You can't forget a biometric – it's your finger or eye scan **(1)**.

### Module 29: Ethics

1. Answers to include:
   - Definition of the right to be forgotten – that individuals have the right – under certain conditions – to ask.
   - Search engines to remove links with personal information about them.
   - Current news about people who have been reported as using this right (such as Mario Costeja Gonzalez, who provided the test case).
   - Clearly supported reasoning behind opinion, e.g.
     - Innocent people shouldn't have to drag around incorrect online stories
     - The Internet doesn't forget
     - Internet searches help check on prospective employees or partners

   **[6 marks: 0–2 marks – A poor response containing little justification for the argument. No use of technical language and poor use of spelling and grammar; 3–4 marks – A response is given that relates to the scenario. Some justification for the argument. Some examples are provided and there is some use of technical language. Only minor errors in spelling and grammar; 5–6 marks – A detailed response is given that is related to the scenario. Detailed justification for the argument. There is a balanced discussion and all examples are relevant and appropriate. There are few, if any, errors in spelling and grammar.]**

2. Define Internet of Things: the network of physical objects or 'things' embedded with electronics, software, sensors, and connectivity to the Internet.
   Argument (positive or negative) including evidence such as:
   - A smart home helps people who are disabled live a more 'normal' or mainstream life.
   - When computers monitor presence in a home and can be hacked – is this a privacy concern?
   - If your fridge can keep a watch and report to your doctor on how much chocolate you eat – does this erode your individual rights to eat what you choose?
   - If your phone can check your heart rate if you are at risk of a heart attack, or it can check if you're about to suffer an epileptic fit – doesn't that reassure you and your family?

   **[6 marks: 0–2 marks – A poor response containing little justification for the argument. No use of technical language and poor use of spelling and grammar; 3–4 marks – A response is given that relates to the scenario. Some justification for the argument. Some examples are provided and there is some use of technical language. Only minor errors in spelling and grammar; 5–6 marks – A detailed response is given that is related to the scenario. Detailed justification for the argument. There is a balanced discussion and all examples are relevant and appropriate. There are few, if any, errors in spelling and grammar.]**

3. Answers to include elements such as:
   - The owner of the servers might be bought out or go bankrupt: what happens to your data?
   - The servers might be hacked.
   - The legal framework might change of the country where the data is stored – e.g. 'safe harbor' rules of the US and the 2015 EU decision to not accept this.
   - Online storage allows data files to be accessed from anywhere with online access.
   - Online storage allows collaboration between colleagues on one file.

   **[6 marks: 0–2 marks – A poor response containing little justification for the argument. No use of technical language and poor use of spelling and grammar; 3–4 marks – A response is given that relates to the scenario. Some justification for the argument. Some examples are provided and there is some use of technical language. Only minor errors in spelling and grammar; 5–6 marks – A detailed response is given that is related to the scenario. Detailed justification for the argument. There is a balanced discussion and all examples are relevant and appropriate. There are few, if any, errors in spelling and grammar.]**

4. Answers to include elements such as:
   - Data should be fairly and lawfully processed.
   - Data should only be used or disclosed for the specified notified purposes.
   - Data should be adequate, relevant and not excessive.
   - Data should be accurate and kept up to date.
   - Data should not be kept any longer than necessary.
   - Access must be provided for individuals to check and correct their data, with a right of explanation when a computer takes automated decisions based on the data.
   - Data should not be transferred outside the European Union except to countries with adequate data protection legislation.

   **[6 marks: 0–2 marks – A poor response containing little justification for the argument. No use of technical language and poor use of spelling and grammar; 3–4 marks – A response is given that relates to the scenario. Some justification for the argument. Some examples are provided and there is some use of technical language. Only minor errors in spelling and grammar; 5–6 marks – A detailed response is given that is related to the scenario. Detailed justification for the argument. There is a balanced discussion and all examples are relevant and appropriate. There are few, if any, errors in spelling and grammar.]**

### Module 30: Encryption

1. This is a simple 'shift' cipher, whereby each letter represents another in a logical sequence **(1)**.
2. GCSE COMPUTER SCIENCE **(1)**
3. Hashing is used to check whether anyone has tried to break the code before sending it on. Any changes to anything in the content will produce a garbled or changed message when the legitimate key is used **(1)**.
4. Plaintext is an unencrypted message **(1)**.
5. Encrypted data is deliberately scrambled so that it cannot be understood straight off **(1)**. The unauthorised person would not have the key to decrypt the data **(1)**.
6. Answers to include:
   E-commerce
   Online banking
   Secure messaging
   Government business
   **[2 marks: 1 mark for each use identified]**
7. SSL stands for 'secure sockets layer', a protocol that uses a key to encrypt data **(1)** across the Internet using two keys: a public key accessible to all and a private key known only to the recipient of the message **(1)**. This combination is the only way in which secure communication is possible **(1)**. Your browser connects to the website and requests an identity check from the server, to make sure that the server sends a recognised SSL certificate. If this is part of a list the browser holds, then all is well. If not, the browser will ask the user 'Are you sure you want to deal with the owners of this website? I don't know them!' At this point it is a good idea to pause and check you have typed the correct URL, because this is a hint that something isn't necessarily right. If the certificate is recognised, the URL changes from HTTP to HTTPS and you can continue your session in an encrypted mode **(1)**.

**Paper 1**

1. 151 **(1)**
2. 1111101 **(1)**
3. cache ✓ **(1)**
4. **a)** A Caesar cipher is a set of alphabetical letters set against a second set, but 'shifted' a set number of places so that each letter is paired against a different one in the opposing set **(1)**. When a message is encoded, the coded letters (not the original message) are sent to the recipient, who can decode the message only if they know the 'shift' **(1)**.

   **b)**

   | P | B | Z | C | H | G | R | E | F |  | H | F | R |
   |---|---|---|---|---|---|---|---|---|---|---|---|---|
   | C | O | M | P | U | T | E | R | S |  | U | S | E |
   | O | V | A | N | E | L |   |   |   |   |   |   |   |
   | B | I | N | A | R | Y |   |   |   |   |   |   |   |

   **[3 marks: 1 mark for each correct word decoded]**
5. **a)** A client-server model spreads the workload between the main server and the user's device **(1)**.

   **b)** A client device may share resources with the more powerful server **(1)**, which enables faster communication because the server does the work before transmission **(1)**.
6. Hexadecimal is easier for humans to read ✓ **(1)**
7. 58,34,2,4,39,54,1 = starting

   34, 58   2,4   54,39  1

          2,4   34,58  39,54,1

        1,2,4,34,39,54,58 = finishing

   **[2 marks: 1 mark for correct steps, 1 mark for correct outcome]**
8. **a)**

   | target | found | i | list[i] |
   |--------|-------|---|---------|
   | 30 | false | 1 | 2 |
   |  |  | 2 | 3 |
   |  |  | 3 | 5 |
   |  |  | 4 | 7 |
   |  |  | 5 | 30 |
   |  | true | 6 | 35 |
   |  |  |  |  |

   **[4 marks: 1 mark for each correct column]**

   **b)** `WHILE i<=6 AND found = false` ✓ **(1)**
9. Example answer:

   ```
   IF hour = 0 THEN
        OUTPUT 12
        OUTPUT 'am'
   ELSE    IF hour < 12 THEN
        OUTPUT hour
        OUTPUT 'am'
   ELSE       IF hour = 12 THEN
        OUTPUT 12
        OUTPUT 'pm'
   ELSE       hour ← hour - 12
              OUTPUT hour
              OUTPUT 'pm'
              ENDIF
        ENDIF
   ENDIF
   ```
   **(4)**
10. **a)**

    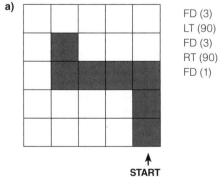

    FD (3)
    LT (90)
    FD (3)
    RT (90)
    FD (1)

    **START** (2)

    **b)** FD (3)
    LT (90)
    FD (2)
    RT (90)
    FD (2)
    LT (90)
    FD (2) **(2)**
11.

    | Character | Huffman coding |
    |-----------|----------------|
    | SPACE | 111 |
    | N | 00011 |
    | A | 001 |

    **[3 marks: 1 mark for each correct row]**
12. **a)** WarehouseLocation **(1)**

    **b)** 5 **(1)**

    **c)** The primary key **(1)** from Warehouse is a field in the Stock table **(1)**.
13. **a)** Each bit can hold two colours **(1)** – 36 pixels in a two-colour image need 36 bits **(1)**.

    **b)** 2 per pixel **(1)**
14. Resolution is the number of pixels per set size, e.g. per inch, not in the overall image **(1)**.
15. An operating system manages the computer resources and is the interface between the user and the computer **(1)**. It controls memory and processing time, manages access rights of users and handles errors **(1)**.
16.   100101

    +   10101

      111010

    **[2 marks: 1 mark for correct working and 1 mark for correct answer]**
17. Character ✓ **(1)**

    Boolean ✓ **(1)**
18. 16,21,11,19 -> 16,11,19,21 -> 11,16,19,21 **[3 marks: 1 mark for each stage. Mark for last stage will only be awarded when the other stages are correct]**
19. 10 ✓ **(1)**
20. The worst situation for bubble sort is when the list is effectively in reversed order, so that every element **(1)** is in the 'wrong' position **(1)** and must be moved on each pass so that the sort will need to make the maximum number of passes **(1)** through the list.
21. Example answers:

    ```
    Set total to zero
    Set score counter to one
    While score counter is less than or equal to ten
         Input the next score
         Add the score into the total
    Set the class average to the total divided by ten
    Print the class average.
    ```

    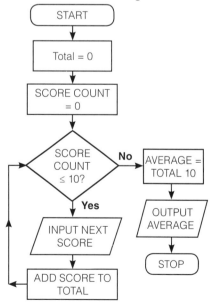

    **[4 marks: 1 mark for right sequence, 1 mark for loop, 1 mark for accurate calculation, 1 mark for output]**

22. Position (or index) 4 **(1)**
23. Arrays are of fixed size, so they cannot be edited without rewriting the code. ✓
    Arrays can only store data of one type. ✓ **[1 mark: both correct for 1 mark]**
24. Array **(1)**
    Boolean **(1)**
25. Any two from: to make code easier to read; to allow for code reuse/sharing; to improve code maintenance/make the code easier to update; to reduce programmer error. **[2 marks: 1 mark for each answer]**
26. The data sent to a function by the subroutine that called it ✓ **(1)**
27. Logic error ✓ **(1)**
28. Answers to include:
    High-level languages are human readable, but must be compiled or interpreted to be processed by the computer. Low-level languages are closer to machine code, but are hard for humans to read.
    If you write in a low-level language you have much more control over the performance of the code and processor, while in a high-level language you are dependent on the compiler. If you write in a high-level language you can more easily debug an error track it, since it is easier for humans to read.
    Low-level languages take longer to write and check than high-level languages, but writing code in high-level languages loses some of the time benefit because the code must be compiled.
    Low-level languages are harder for humans to learn than high-level languages.
    **[6 marks: 1–2 marks: There are a few simple or vague statements relating to the question. The form and style of writing has many deficiencies. Ideas are not often clearly expressed. Sentences and paragraphs are often not well-connected or at times bullet points may have been used. Specialist vocabulary has been used inappropriately or not at all. Much of the text is legible and some of the meaning is clear. There are many errors of spelling, punctuation and grammar but it should still be possible to understand much of the response. 3–4 marks: There is evidence of some evaluation shown through the use of mostly correct technical explanation linked with advantages in the situation given. The answer covers a few of the ideas above or includes other correct answers. The form and style of writing is appropriate to the purpose and some complex ideas are expressed reasonably clearly and fluently. Well linked sentences and paragraphs are usually used. Specialist vocabulary has been used on a number of occasions but not always appropriately. Text is legible and most of the meaning is clear. There are occasional errors of spelling, punctuation and grammar. 5–6 marks: There is evidence of a clear evaluation shown by a correct explanation and three well justified comments. The answer covers most of the ideas above or includes other correct answers. The form and style of writing is appropriate to the purpose and complex ideas are expressed clearly and fluently. Sentences and paragraphs follow on from one another clearly and coherently. Specialist vocabulary has been used appropriately throughout. Text is legible and the meaning is clear. There are few, if any, errors of spelling, punctuation and grammar.]**

**Paper 2**

1. Answers to include:
   A bus network has a central spine of network cabling (called a bus) while a ring network has all of the computers connected to each other in a circle.
   A bus network is simple and cheapest to install and is good for a temporary network. It is flexible because elements can be removed or added without messing with the rest of the network. It is best used in small or temporary networks and can be a useful home network solution. A ring network can offer fast data flow when it is working well – all data flows in one direction. Even when the load is the same, this performs better than a bus setup. Each device can access the resources on the network equally.
   Both have disadvantages, however. In a bus network, if the bus (spine) fails the whole network crashes. Performance is affected by load so the more devices attached, the slower it functions. Bus cables are limited in length, so the network is limited in size, and must be terminated properly to avoid reflection of signal, which can crash the system. Data has to 'queue' sometimes because the bus is busy with other demands. In a ring network, each packet of data has to travel through all of the devices between its origin and its destination. If one device malfunctions the whole network is compromised. Setting this up is more expensive than a bus network. **[5 marks: 1 mark for each correct point made]**
2. A LAN is a network in which all connected devices are relatively close together **(1)**, in a single building or premises, like a school or office complex **(1)**. A WAN, on the other hand, is a network in which the connected devices are too thinly spread to make a physical connection **(1)**. These tend to be connected through telephone lines, undersea cables and, in extreme cases, satellite links **(1)**.
3. Answers to include:
   A wired network offers a more reliable connection because the link is physical. This means that it is also usually faster than wireless connections. It is less convenient because it ties the device to one place, but because the data is transferred through a physical link it is more secure.
   A wireless network allows more freedom of movement, although you can lose signal under less than ideal conditions. Sharing a wireless access point with other users can also slow the speed of any data transfer. Security can be an issue since data is broadcast rather than contained within a cable.
   **[6 marks: 1–2 marks: There are a few simple or vague statements relating to the question. The form and style of writing has many deficiencies. Ideas are not often clearly expressed. Sentences and paragraphs are often not well-connected or at times bullet points may have been used. Specialist vocabulary has been used inappropriately or not at all. Much of the text is legible and some of the meaning is clear. There are many errors of spelling, punctuation and grammar but it should still be possible to understand much of the response. 3–4 marks: There is evidence of some evaluation shown through the use of mostly correct technical explanation linked with advantages in the situation given. The answer covers a few of the ideas above or includes other correct answers. The form and style of writing is appropriate to the purpose and some complex ideas are expressed reasonably clearly and fluently. Well linked sentences and paragraphs are usually used. Specialist vocabulary has been used on a number of occasions but not always appropriately.**

Answers

Text is legible and most of the meaning is clear. There are occasional errors of spelling, punctuation and grammar. 5–6 marks: There is evidence of a clear evaluation shown by a correct explanation and three well justified comments. The answer covers most of the ideas above or includes other correct answers. The form and style of writing is appropriate to the purpose and complex ideas are expressed clearly and fluently. Sentences and paragraphs follow on from one another clearly and coherently. Specialist vocabulary has been used appropriately throughout. Text is legible and the meaning is clear. There are few, if any, errors of spelling, punctuation and grammar.]

4.

| APPLICATION LAYER |
| --- |

| TRANSPORT LAYER |
| --- |

| INTERNET LAYER |
| --- |

| NETWORK ACCESS (or DATA LINK) LAYER |
| --- |

[3 marks: 1 mark for each correct layer]

5.  IMAP ✓ (1)
6.  5 megabits per second = 5 000 000 bits per second (3)
7.

| A | B | D | K | Z |
| --- | --- | --- | --- | --- |
| 0 | 0 | 0 | 0 | 1 |
| 0 | 1 | 1 | 1 | 0 |
| 1 | 0 | 1 | 0 | 1 |
| 1 | 1 | 1 | 1 | 0 |

[6 marks: 2 marks for each correct column]

8.  a)  An embedded system is part of a larger system, such as traffic lights, and is designed to work without human intervention. Usually the 'computer' part is invisible to the user (1).
    b)  Any one from: senses cloth quality and density to identify quantity of water needed; detect water temperature; manage wash cycle (1).

9.

| A | B | A AND B |
| --- | --- | --- |
| 0 | 0 | 0 |
| 0 | 1 | 0 |
| 1 | 0 | 0 |
| 1 | 1 | 1 | (1)

10.

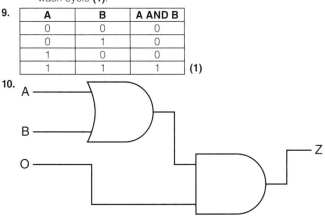

[3 marks: 1 mark for A and B into an OR gate, 1 mark for O and the output of A and B into an AND gate, 1 mark for the output of the gate with O as an input with its output connected to Z]

11.  Cloud storage is the term for storing your data on computer systems belonging to someone else, and accessing them through the Internet (1). Advantages of cloud storage include that you may access them from anywhere with an Internet connection (1), and can therefore collaborate with people regardless of distance or time. Local disaster recovery is easier too, since you can restore from an online backup (1). Costs are generally lower per MB than local storage (1). On the other hand, however, your data is stored on someone else's computer, so you need to be sure of their security measures (1), and of ownership of your data should that company be bought or go into bankruptcy. Moving what can be considerable amounts of data from one provider to another can also cause problems (1).

12.  Both file types use compression to reduce file size (1) and therefore people may be concerned about the loss of quality as both remove either image elements or certain audio frequencies (1).

13.  It is most effective on images with many continuous pixels of the same colour ✓ (1)

14.  Text data ✓ (1)

15.  System software ✓ (1)

16.  Instructions are close to English/easier for humans to read and write than a low-level language, which means a programmer is less likely to make errors (1). It's quicker to develop code and easier to maintain high level code (1). High-level languages are usually available across many platforms or chipsets or operating systems (1).

17.  You can come to either stance but you need to use evidence to support your response. Answers to include:
The advantages of using subroutines over writing the code repeatedly as needed include clearly breaking a big task into little ones makes the big task more achievable. Using code modules or subroutines (one for each part of the task) makes it easy to see which part of the code does which part of the overall task. Updates are a lot easier – you just change the bit that needs to be updated. A subroutine may work perfectly one time that it is called, but the main code may then change the variable used by the subroutine – and the subroutine may fail. Finally, testing through the entire code checking, each iteration of each subroutine, can feel like an endless task. [6 marks: 1 mark for each point made]

18.  A patch will fix any known security issues (1) so the machine running the application is less vulnerable to cyberattack (1).

19.  A way of organising data so that it can be used efficiently ✓ (1)

20.  Answers to include: Backup (ideally off-site) to help make sure that if data is corrupted in some way the copy may be used; Passwords to ensure only authorised people gain access to the data; Access levels to help ensure that only the right people gain access to editing or creation options; Redundancy – keeping a parallel system (or resources) running ready to take over if anything happens to the main system (or resources).
[6 marks: 1–2 marks: There are a few simple or vague statements relating to the question. The form and style of writing used has many deficiencies. Ideas are not often clearly expressed. Sentences and paragraphs are often not well-connected or at times bullet points may have been used. Specialist vocabulary has been used inappropriately or not at all. Much of the text is legible and some of the meaning is clear. There are many errors of spelling, punctuation and grammar but it should still be possible to understand much of the response. 3–4 marks: There is evidence of some evaluation shown through the use of mostly correct technical explanation linked with advantages in the situation given. The answer covers a few of the ideas above or includes other correct answers. The form and style

style of writing used is appropriate to purpose and expresses some complex ideas reasonably clearly and fluently. Well linked sentences and paragraphs are usually used. Specialist vocabulary has been used on a number of occasions but not always appropriately. Text is legible and most of the meaning is clear. There are occasional errors of spelling, punctuation and grammar. 5–6 marks: There is evidence of a clear evaluation shown by a correct explanation and three well justified comments. The answer covers most of the ideas above or includes other correct answers. A form and style of writing appropriate to purpose is used and complex ideas are expressed clearly and fluently. Sentences and paragraphs follow on from one another clearly and coherently. Specialist vocabulary has been used appropriately throughout. Text is legible and the meaning is clear. There are few if any errors of spelling, punctuation and grammar.]**

21. **a)** Validation is an automatic computer check to ensure that the data entered is sensible and reasonable **(1)**.
    **b)** Any two from: check digit; format check; length check; lookup limit; presence check; range check
    **[2 marks: 1 mark for each correct answer]**

22. A variable is data stored in memory that can be changed. ✓

23. Normal (or typical) **(1)**: e.g. 07625738925 **(1)**
    Extreme (or boundary) **(1)**: 07000000000 or 07999999999 **(1)**
    Erroneous **(1)**: e.g. Sheffield71155 **(1)**

Notes

Notes